Mending Handbook
Repair & Restore Fabric & Textiles
SHANNON ROUDHÁN and
JASON BOWLSBY
I0824304
stashBOOKS
an imprint of C&T Publishing

Publisher: Amy Barrett-Daffin

Creative Director: Gailen Runge

Senior Editor: Roxane Cerda

Technical Editor: Debbie Rodgers

Cover/Book Designer: April Mostek

Production Coordinator: Tim Manibusan

Illustrator: Kirstie Pettersen

Photography Coordinator: Rachel Ackley

Front cover photography by Jason Bowlsby

Photography by Jason Bowlsby, unless otherwise noted

Published by Stash Books, an imprint of C&T Publishing, Inc., P.O. Box 1456, Lafayette, CA 94549

Library of Congress Cataloging-in-Publication Data

Names: Roudhán, Shannon Leigh, 1967- author | Bowlsby, Jason, 1970- author

Title: Mending handbook : repair & restore fabric & textiles / Shannon Roudhán and Jason Bowlsby.

Description: Lafayette, CA : Stash Books, an imprint of C&T Publishing, [2026] | Summary: "Refresh your wardrobe with detailed instructions and 50 embroidery and mending stitches. Explore tips for tricky fabrics, creative fixes, and no-sew solutions, ensuring you're ready for any repair"-- Provided by publisher.

Identifiers: LCCN 2025040139 | ISBN 9781644035788 trade paperback | ISBN 9781644035795 ebook

Subjects: LCSH: Repairing | Reweaving | BISAC: CRAFTS & HOBBIES / Needlework / Embroidery | CRAFTS & HOBBIES / Fashion

Classification: LCC TT151 .R683 2026 | DDC 643/.7--dc23/eng/20250929

LC record available at https://lccn.loc.gov/2025040139

Printed in China

10 9 8 7 6 5 4 3 2 1

CONTENTS

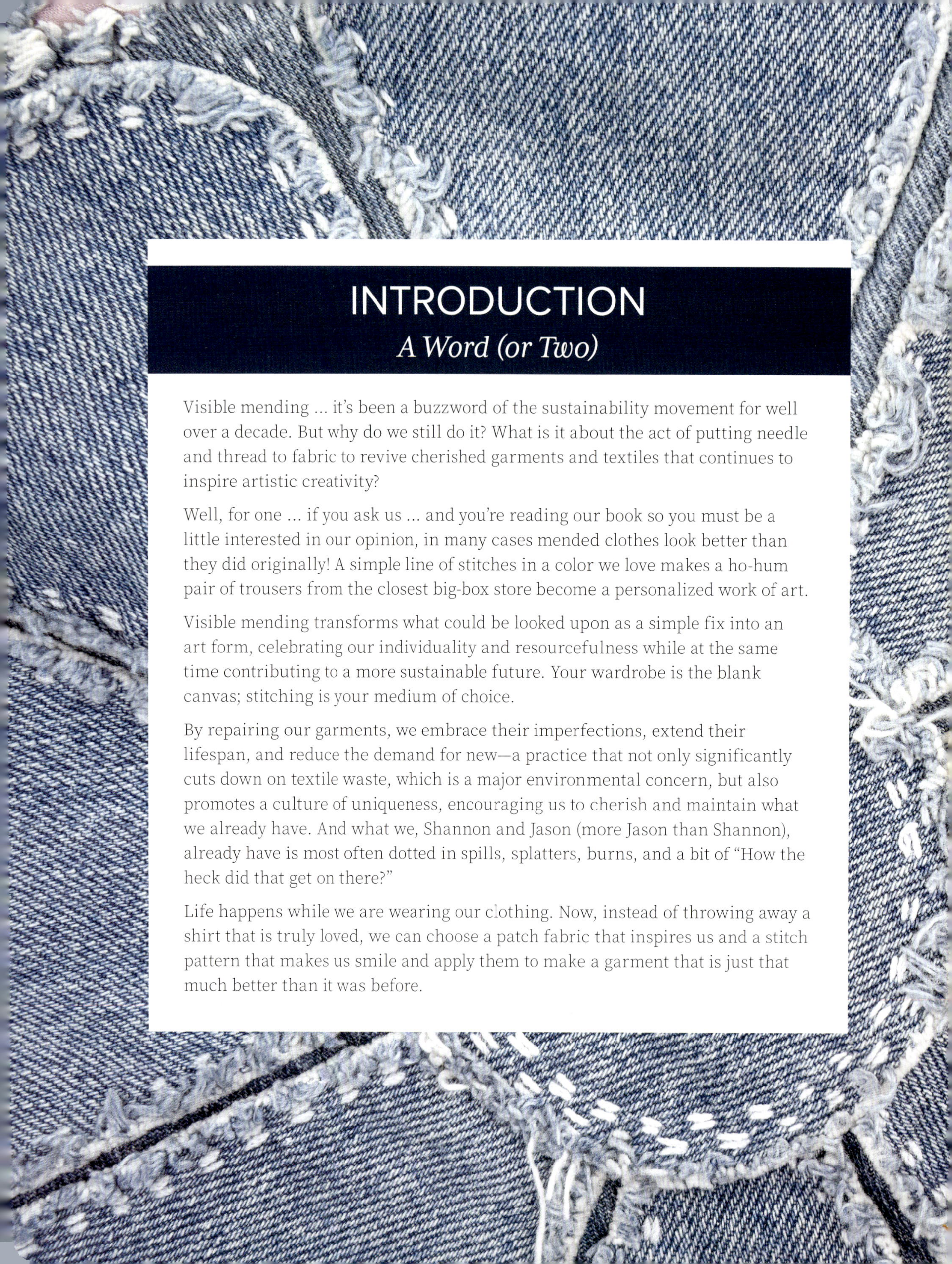

INTRODUCTION

A Word (or Two)

Visible mending ... it's been a buzzword of the sustainability movement for well over a decade. But why do we still do it? What is it about the act of putting needle and thread to fabric to revive cherished garments and textiles that continues to inspire artistic creativity?

Well, for one ... if you ask us ... and you're reading our book so you must be a little interested in our opinion, in many cases mended clothes look better than they did originally! A simple line of stitches in a color we love makes a ho-hum pair of trousers from the closest big-box store become a personalized work of art.

Visible mending transforms what could be looked upon as a simple fix into an art form, celebrating our individuality and resourcefulness while at the same time contributing to a more sustainable future. Your wardrobe is the blank canvas; stitching is your medium of choice.

By repairing our garments, we embrace their imperfections, extend their lifespan, and reduce the demand for new—a practice that not only significantly cuts down on textile waste, which is a major environmental concern, but also promotes a culture of uniqueness, encouraging us to cherish and maintain what we already have. And what we, Shannon and Jason (more Jason than Shannon), already have is most often dotted in spills, splatters, burns, and a bit of "How the heck did that get on there?"

Life happens while we are wearing our clothing. Now, instead of throwing away a shirt that is truly loved, we can choose a patch fabric that inspires us and a stitch pattern that makes us smile and apply them to make a garment that is just that much better than it was before.

THE MENDING KIT

A well-equipped mending kit is a must-have, supplying much needed items without having to search drawers, jars, and baskets for thread, needles, glue, buttons, fabric stabilizers, and other essentials. Assemble these items in one box and keep a separate smaller zipper case with essentials for travel and for traversing everyday life.

NEEDLES

Choosing the correct needle for the job is essential to a successful mend.

Darners

Darning needles are long with large eyes, which makes them perfect for thicker threads and yarn. They are also heavy-duty needles, so they are ideal for heavier fabrics. We use long darning needles for sashiko.

Sharps and Betweens

Sharps and betweens are generally what most folx think of when they think of hand-sewing needles. Both needles have sharp points and come in a variety of lengths and thicknesses. Sharps are slightly longer than betweens, and keeping on hand a variety pack of each is smart.

Sashiko

Sashiko needles have large eyes for handling thicker threads and are long with a long, tapered tip. Because they are usually more difficult to find, we end up reaching for long darning needles more often than not.

Bent Tip

Bent-tip needles are particularly good for working with yarn or for weaving through yarn and fabric. Bent-tip needles come with either blunt tips or sharp tips, depending on the fabric and thread or yarn you are working with.

Tapestry or Cross Stitch

These needles have a blunt tip, which makes them ideal for weaving, yarn stitching, and working stitches through fabric with a more open weave to prevent piercing the fabric or the underlying threads.

Chenille

Chenille needles have large eyes and sharp tips, making them perfect for working with thicker threads and yarn. They are quite sturdy, making them good for heavy fabrics.

Variety Packs

Nothing beats a good variety pack of needles to keep on hand, and we have just about one of everything. Packs can be found specifically for crafting, household mending, and hand sewing. Especially if hand sewing is a new undertaking, these packs can be a good way to explore different needle types and they come in HAND-y (see what we did there?) for when those odd tasks arise. And there are always odd tasks arising around here … just sayin'.

Variety pack of needles from the Colonial Needle Company

Curved and Specialty

There are times and places when a standard needle just won't do the job. This is where specialty needles come into play. Whether you are sewing at an awkward angle, using thick material, or even patching your couch, look for a needle that is designed just for that task.

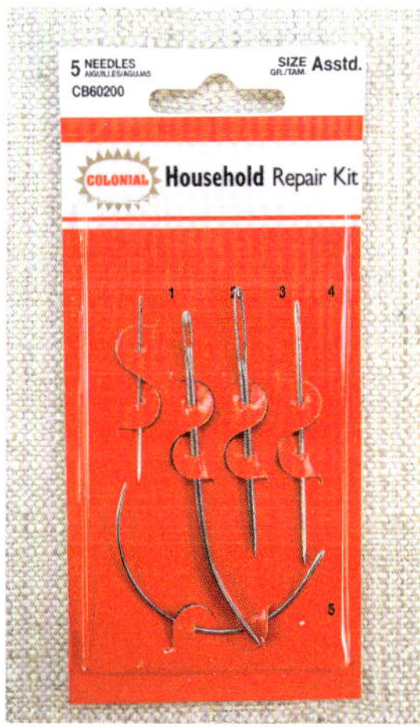

Colonial Needle Company Household Repair Kit

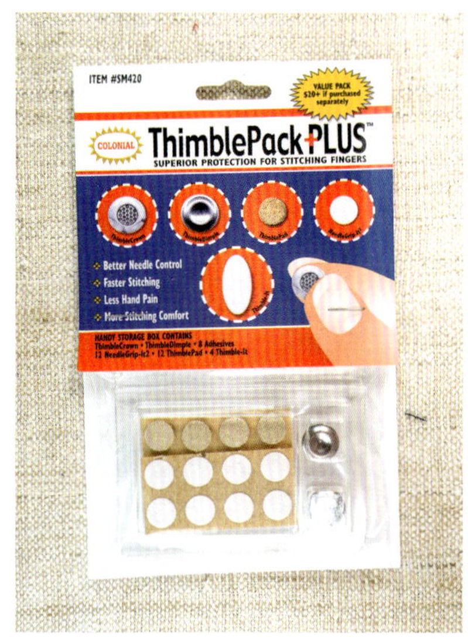

THIMBLES

Traditional fingertip thimbles cover the entire finger pad, protecting it from needle pricks and providing a surface to push from. There are dozens of styles to choose from. Try a few and see what feels best on your hands.

Palm Thimbles

This specialized thimble is designed to be worn on the palm of your hand, rather than on a fingertip. It's used primarily for pushing needles through thick fabric while sewing, particularly in techniques like sashiko.

Thimble Pads

Used the same way as traditional thimbles, these are smaller disks that stick directly to your fingertip. We use these in areas where we need more dexterity. Again, there is a wide variety to choose from, ranging from dimpled metal to soft and slightly tacky, enabling you to pull needles through fabric with more ease.

THREAD, FLOSS, AND YARN

Thread, floss, and *yarn* are interchangeable terms, and their use depends on the desired textural result and the base fabric being mended. There is a larger discussion that could be had regarding the differences in and uses of these three products, but we will discuss them here as they specifically apply to mending.

Thread

Thread has multiple strands of fibers spun together into a single strand and is designed to be used as is without separating the strands from one another.

It is easily found in a wide variety of fibers such as cotton, wool, polyester, or nylon, and in an assortment of thicknesses, each suited to a different function. Thread is your go-to for woven fabric mends.

Floss

Floss is multiple strands of thread plied together that can be used as is or separated and used in combinations of a number of strands or color combinations. Floss is ideal for woven fabric mends.

Yarn

Yarn is typically used for knitting, crocheting, and weaving, but it's also used in mending both woven and knit textiles. Sizes, fibers, and textures are incredibly varied and fun to use for adding texture to stitches and designs. We recommend reaching for yarn first when mending knits.

MARKING TOOLS

Marking tools help define the mending area, ensuring your stitching is intentional and aesthetically pleasing. They help provide a clear boundary for decorative stitches, making the repair more noticeable (or less noticeable if that's your thing). Essentially, they help turn the mend into a deliberate artistic element instead of just a fix.

Be sure to test any marking tools for visibility and removal on a piece of identical fabric before you mark!

Erasable Marking Pen

For marking on dark fabrics.

Washable Markers

Washable markers are inexpensive and work beautifully on a wide array of fabrics.

Hera Marker

These small plastic, wood, or bone tools make nonpermanent creases in the fabric that can be washed away. These are especially useful for marking grids and patterns. Don't have a Hera Marker? Use the back of a butter knife!

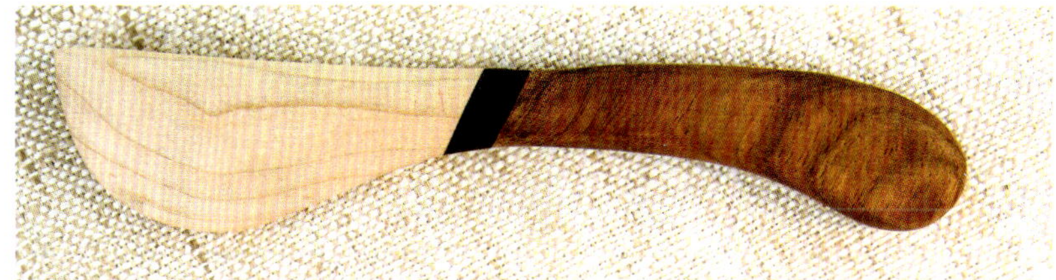

OTHER ESSENTIAL TOOLS

Scissors

A must for your kit! Whether you are trimming threads or cutting fabric, scissors are one of the first tools you will need.

Crochet Hooks

For working on runs or snags in knits. These come in a variety of sizes, so having a few will assist your mending.

Stitch Markers

For holding yarn loops in place on knits.

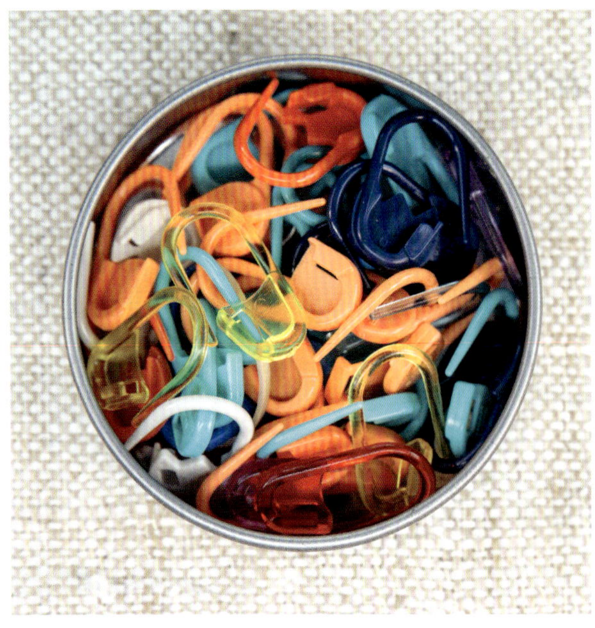

Darning Mushroom and Eggs

These tools are used to mend holes and tears in woven cloth and knitwear and are particularly useful when applied to fabrics with stretch. They provide a stable surface for mending, allowing stitches to be made easily. Other options include:

- A small jar or jar lid
- A wide-mouth canning jar ring
- A round disk
- A darning mushroom with a groove for adding a rubber band to hold the fabric in place
- A darning stick (for gloves)
- A darning loom (check out the Speedweve, originally released in the 1940s)

Embroidery Hoops

An embroidery hoop is a tool used to hold fabric taut while stitching on it. It consists of two rings, one inside the other, with the fabric sandwiched between them. They come in a wide range of sizes, so it is easy to find a size that fits the mend.

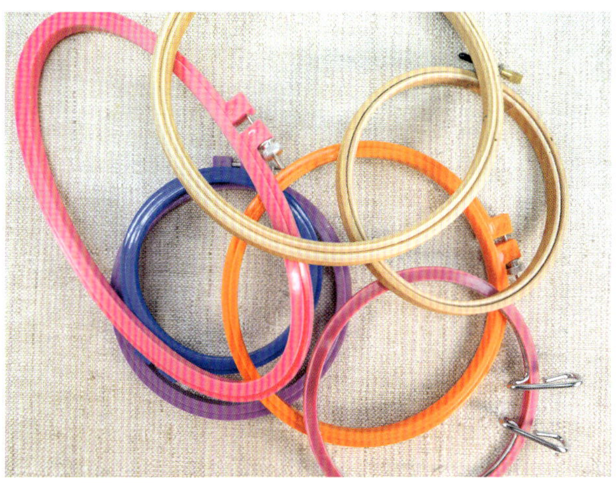

Rubber Bands/Hair Bands

These are great for securing fabric onto a jar or mason jar ring.

Scraps of Fabric for Patches

An assortment of fabric scraps make patching on the go a breeze.

Buttons

Collect a couple of dark, light, and something in between to act as a temporary place holder in case of emergencies until an exact match can be found.

STABILIZERS AND GLUE

Keeping your work steady and straight will give you much better results. From basting patches to stabilizing slinky fabric, stabilizers and glues are going to make your life that much easier.

Stabilizer

Stabilizer is a sheet of material that keeps fabric flat and smooth while embroidering or mending. It's a key component of visible mending, especially useful for stretchy fabrics. Stabilizer comes in myriad forms including iron-on or sew-in; water-soluble, cutaway, or tearaway; and in sheets, packs, rolls, or cut off the bolt.

Liquid Stabilizer or Fabric Stiffener

Another option is a water-soluble solution that can be applied directly to fabric to temporarily stiffen the fabric. This type of product provides support during the mending process, preventing puckering, and ensures smooth stitching, but it washes away easily.

Glue and Fusible Webbing

Fabric glue and fusible webbing are specialized products designed specifically for bonding different types of fabric together, allowing fabrics to join without sewing. Types include permanent (which bonds to the fabric and remains, useful for hems and joining fabric) and temporary (which washes away or wears away over time, great for basting a patch in place before sewing it down).

Permanent fabric glues

Permanent fusible web

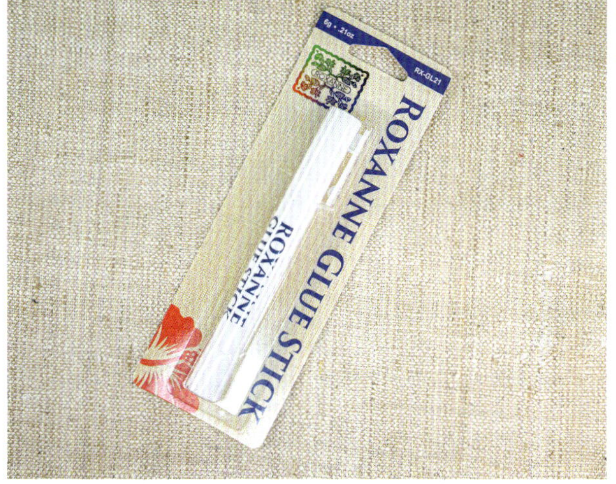

Washable glue stick

Roxanne Temporary Adhesive Spray glue

Metric Conversions

The metric measurements in this book follow standard conversion practices for sewing and soft crafts. The metric equivalents are often rounded off for ease of use. If you need more exact measurements, there are a number of amazing online converters.

PREP THE MEND

PREPARE TO SUCCEED

No matter how good the stitching is, if the fabric is not prepared properly, the mend will not be secure. Before those first stitches are made or the first layer of fusible is applied, be sure to assess the situation carefully to decide if stitches alone will do or if stitches and a patch are needed. Is the damage a snag, tear, hole, burn, stain, or rip? Is the fabric wearing thin? Do you need to reinforce the fabric around the area to be mended before applying a patch or stitching? Take a moment to consider what the fabric looks like now and what it should look like when the mend is complete. Then prep the fabric and start stitching!

The easiest assessment to make is whether the fabric is woven or knit. Both have a wide range of mending options, but knowing which type of fabric you are working with will set the path for the rest of the mend.

WOVEN PREP

Woven fabric is made up of threads running in two directions. First, a layer of threads (called *warp threads*) are set in place, all running in one direction vertically. Next, a set of threads (called *weft threads*) are woven over and under those warp threads horizontally, creating the fabric. Depending on the density of the woven fabric in need of repair and depending on the type of thread used to create the fabric, the edges of a hole will have frayed or ragged edges. The choice here is whether to clean those up or not.

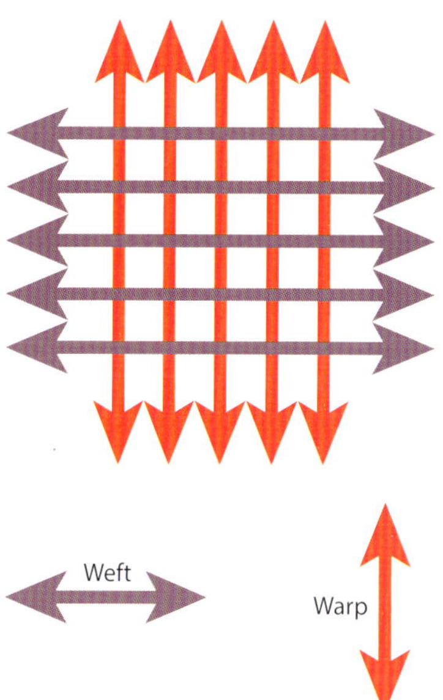

Sometimes we love the look of a frayed edge with a patch behind the mend.

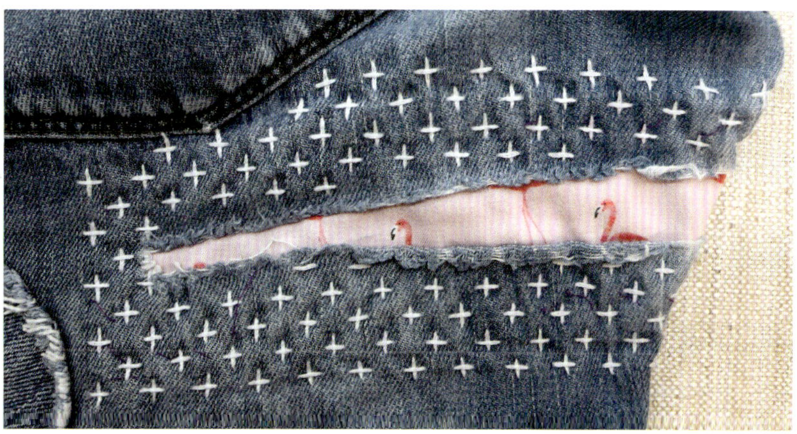

Other times, we prefer cleaning up the edges of the hole before patching.

For a frayed edge, all that is needed is to cut away any unwanted threads and trim the remaining threads to length. It all depends on if you are going for an '80s rock legend look or something a bit more tame. It's up to you.

Once the desired amount of frayed chaos is achieved, a patch or stitches can be applied.

Sometimes a top patch is the desired effect, so the hole is not visible. In this case, a quick cleanup of the edges is needed.

1. For a cleaner edge, cut away all frayed edges, including a bit of the fabric. *fig. A*

2. From the back of the mend, turn the edges in and secure with a bit of fabric glue or a bit of fusible webbing. *fig. B*

Once the edge is turned under and pressed into place, a patch or stitches can be applied.

A.

B.

KNITS PREP

Knit fabric is created from a continuous length of yarn. Live loops are drawn up one row at a time and held in place with a knitting needle for hand knits or held on hooks in the case of machine knits. Each subsequent row is made of loops pulled through the live loops of the previous row until the desired amount of fabric is made. The last row is secured with a series of bound-off stitches that are looped through one another from one side to the other. The challenge with mends in knit fabrics is this single line of yarn that, once broken or damaged, cannot be remade as easily as woven fabric. Once a section of the yarn is broken, the stitches it was attached to will begin to unravel creating runs and holes that can appear quickly and expand aggressively if not caught right away.

In the case of most knit repairs, there is a hole that has been created by a snag or a critter chewing, as a critter does. If a stretched yarn is the issue, it can usually be tightened back up or secured to the back of the fabric (see Snagged!, page 101). If an actual hole has occurred, there may need to be additional cleanup and reinforcing. With holes in knits, there are broken yarns to deal with and, while this may seem a bit complicated, it does become easier after the first fix. So, take a deep breath and take it one step at a time. In some rare cases, it might be advisable to use a permanent reinforcing fabric behind the hole that is supportive without being too stiff compared to the fabric being mended.

Those broken ends along the sides of a hole are going to need to be woven back into the fabric. In order for the ends to be long enough to weave in, we are going to need to unravel them a bit to the left and right of the break.

1. Start by identifying any live loops and securing them with stitch markers or safety pins. These live loops will be picked up with the mending yarn as the stitches are made. *fig. A*

2. Follow the line of the thread and use a crochet hook or a blunt-tip needle to gently pick out the stitches bit by bit until about one or two inches of yarn is available. How much of a tail is needed will depend on how densely knit the fabric is. If the yarn is big and bulky, more will be needed. If the yarn is thinner, less will be needed. *fig. B*

A.

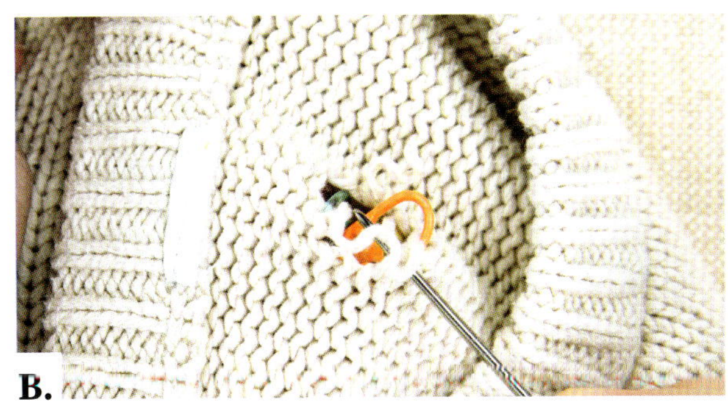

B.

3. As each stitch is unraveled, place a safety pin or a stitch marker in each of the now live stitches to keep them from running. *fig. C*

4. On the back side of the fabric, follow the lines of neighboring stitches and use a yarn needle or tapestry needle to weave the length of the broken tail back into the fabric. *figs. D-E*

5. The ends of these tails can be secured with a bit of permanent fabric glue to prevent them from popping back out and becoming an issue later. *fig. F*

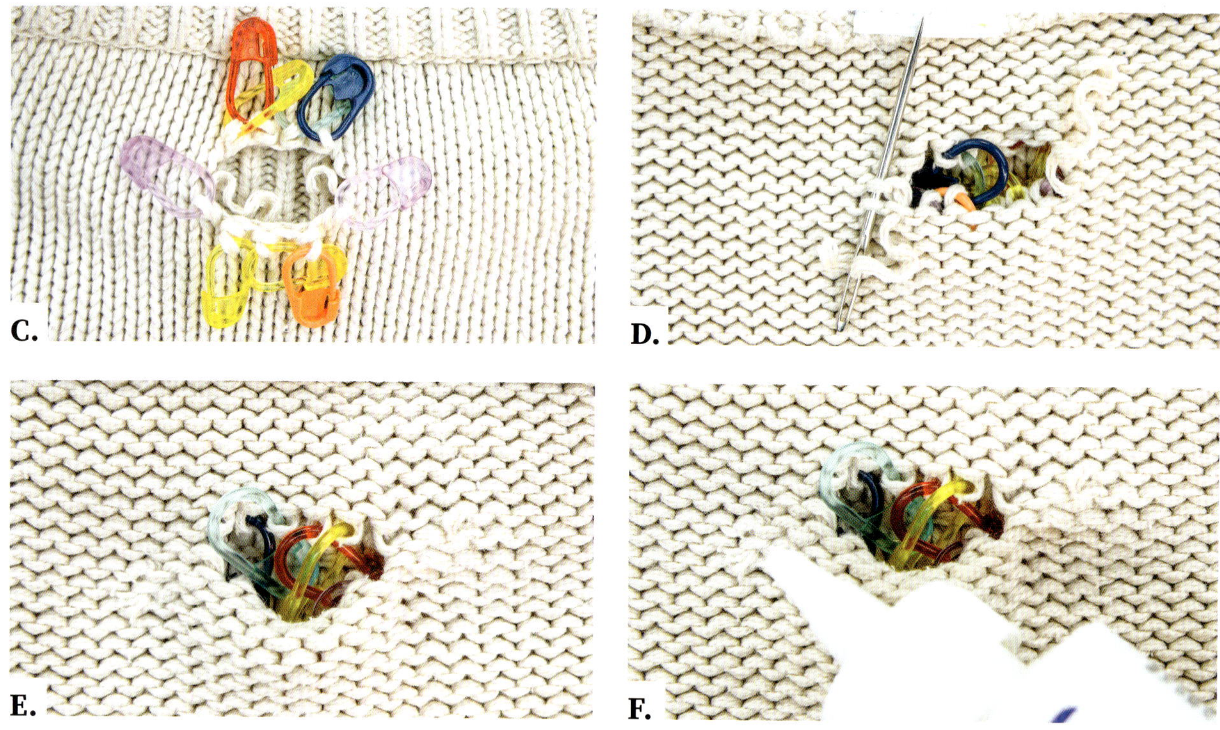

MARKING LINES

For practicing individual stitches, defining a mend area, or for guidelines for stitches such as sashiko or decorative patterns, marking lines are a must. Guidelines ensure precise, even stitches and are especially helpful for more intricate stitches. Further, drawing lines ahead of time is necessary when time is of the essence or the stitching brain just will not engage and we need that extra guidance. We use a variety of products for marking fabric depending on the type and color of the fabric and, in the case of knits, we will use thread to mark the area around a mend if necessary. Regardless of what is used, marking lines are necessary and you should not be shy about using them to keep those stitches neat and tidy.

Marking for Stitch Practice

In the step-outs for stitches, we have made sure to include guide markers to follow where necessary. These are needed for practice but are also practical for the actual mending. Being able to follow the outline of a mend or a design is easier with clear markings. Be sure to look for those markings in the stitch instructions and use them for practice and for application.

Marking a Mend Area

Outlining an area to be mended is a must, especially if a patch is on the back of the fabric. The outline will define the mend area and serve as a guide for stitch placement, ensuring that the mending stitches cover the mend plus about 1″–2″ (2.5–5cm) beyond the mend. Outlining can be done with a pencil, a Hera Marker, the dull side of a kitchen knife, or an erasable or washable fabric pen.

Marking for Sashiko

Sashiko stitches require marked lines (see Marking Lines for Sashiko, page 90).

STITCH INDEX

WHICH STITCH TO PICK

It can be tricky to know which stitches work for the intended mend. Use this table to find just the right stitch for the mend you need to make.

	Appliqué	Basting	Curves	Decorative	Edging	Essentials	Filling Space
Running Stitch (non sashiko) page 28		X				X	
Double Running Stitch page 29						X	
Backstitch pages 30–31					X	X	
Split Stitch pages 32–33					X	X	X
Split Backstitch page 34						X	
Half Backstitch (Open Backstitch) page 35						X	
Outline Stitch pages 36–37			X			X	
Stem Stitch pages 38–39			X			X	
Darning Stitch page 40						X	X
Double Darning Stitch page 41						X	X
Japanese Darning Stitch pages 42–43							X
Chain Stitch pages 44–45			X			X	X
Reverse Chain Stitch pages 46–48			X			X	X
Slip Stitch page 49	X						
Ladder Stitch page 50	X						
Blind Hem Stitch page 51							
Herringbone Stitch (Catch Stitch) page 52				X	X		
Double Herringbone Stitch page 53				X	X		
Whip Stitch page 53					X	X	

	Hemming	Outlining	Reinforcing and Stabilizing	Seams	Securing Patches	Shapes	Knits	Wovens	Hitomezashi Sashiko	Moyouzashi Sashiko
	X	X		X	X		X	X		
		X		X	X		X	X		
		X		X	X		X	X		
		X			X			X		
		X			X			X		
		X			X			X		
		X			X			X		
		X			X			X		
		X	X				X	X		
		X	X		X		X	X		
		X	X		X			X		
		X				X	X	X		
		X				X	X	X		
	X				X			X		
	X				X			X		
	X							X		
	X				X		X	X		
	X				X		X	X		
				X	X		X	X		

Appliqué Stitch page 54	X				X	X		
Blanket Stitch pages 55-57				X	X	X		
Blanket Stitch for Appliqué page 57				X	X	X		
Double Blanket Stitch page 58				X	X			
Blanket Stitch Sunburst pages 58–59				X				
Blanket Stitch Wheel pages 60–61				X				
Tailor's Buttonhole Stitch pages 62-63					X			
Overlock Stitch page 64	X				X			
Offset Running Stitch page 83				X			X	
Offset Crosses page 84				X			X	
Rice Stitch (Sashiko) page 85				X			X	
Diamonds page 87				X			X	
Blue Ocean Waves page 88				X			X	
Asanoha page 89				X			X	
Satin Stitch page 65				X			X	
Brick Stitch page 66				X		X	X	
Feather Stitch pages 66–67				X	X		X	
Detached Chain Stitch page 68				X			X	
Lazy Daisy Stitch page 68				X			X	
Fern Stitch pages 69–70				X	X		X	
French Knot pages 71–72				X			X	
Seed Stitch (Rice Stitch) page 73				X			X	
Star Stitch page 74				X			X	
Weave Stitch page 75				X		X	X	
Spider Wheel (Whipped Wheel) pages 76–77				X			X	
Rose Wheel (Woven Wheel) page 78				X			X	
Back Stitch Trellis page 79				X			X	

				X	X			X		
					X		X	X		
					X			X		
					X	X	X	X		
			X			X	X	X		
			X			X	X	X		
					X			X		
					X		X	X		
			X		X		X	X	X	
			X		X		X	X	X	
			X		X		X	X	X	
			X		X			X		X
			X		X			X		X
			X		X			X		X
								X		
			X					X		
					X		X	X		
					X		X	X		
							X	X		
		X			X		X	X		
			X		X			X		
			X		X			X		
					X			X		
			X		X		X	X		
					X		X	X		
					X		X	X		
			X		X			X		

STITCH DESCRIPTIONS

Hems

It has happened to all of us: The hem of those trousers or that skirt reaches out and hooks itself on a stiletto heel or the edge of a chair or counter, and we feel and hear the rending of stitches from fabric. Now what? First, go to Quick Fixes (page 118) and perform a quick fix with your mending kit. Then, after you're home and able to take needle and thread in hand, use one of these stitches to fix that snagged hem for good.

Essentials

Essentials are the stitches you will draw upon first and often for mending projects. We chose these by thinking about our non-sewing, non-crafty friends and which skills they would need if there were a zombie apocalypse. Reasonable, yes?

Many of these stitches are the basis for other stitches in this book, so we will be referencing them again later on. Learn them and practice them, and don't be afraid to bookmark this section as a quick reference guide.

Edging Stitches

Sure, living on the edge is great but have you ever used stitching to secure or decorate the edge of fabric and patches? That's next level! And these are the stitches you will go to for such greatness.

Decorative

Mending does not mean mundane. As we have said before, mending should elevate the garments and fabric being fixed or reinforced. These decorative stitches will provide endless flexibility for everything from florals to abstracts.

Basting

Basting is not just for the kitchen. Basting stitches are temporary stitches meant to hold a patch in place or to secure layers of fabric while more permanent stitches are applied.

Outlining

Use outlining stitches to define the edges of a mend or to delineate the curves and angles of any shape imaginable.

Securing Patches

Patches can be applied to cover holes, rips, and tears or to hide a stain or burn. They can also be utilized on top of or behind fabric to reinforce a weak spot. In any case, these stitches will do everything from hold down the edges of a patch to securing the central area of a patch or all of the above.

Seams

Put two or more pieces of fabric together, and this set of stitches will make sure they stay together.

Filling Space

Create a shape, and then fill it up for shading or overall texture. Play with these stitches to create depth and textural interest in any mend. Filler stitches are a great way to make sure a patch stays secure or a weak area of fabric is made more stable. Double duty!

Appliqué

Simply put, these stitches enable you to apply a smaller piece of fabric to a larger piece of fabric. Visible or invisible, they all work the same. That patch or fabric panel isn't going anywhere once appliqué stitches do their work.

Reinforcing and Stabilizing

Not every mend is a rip, tear, or burn. Sometimes a well-loved elbow or knee needs somereinforcing, and every now and then the thighs of or the ... ummm ... seat of that favorite pair of jeans needs some shoring up. These stitches work as an allover cure for threadbare and weakened fabric.

Woven

Woven fabric is made of threads running in two directions—the warp and the weft. When those threads weaken, break, or become otherwise damaged, these stitches will be the first to call upon. Read Woven Prep (page 17) first; then come back here and pick your stitches for making your woven fabric all nice and tidy again. Maybe even better than it was before.

Knit

Knit fabric is a unique creature that is created using live and bound-off loops of thread. Once one of those threads is damaged or breaks, they like to run away and leave absolutely frightening-looking slashes and gashes in the fabric. Don't panic! Read Knits Prep (page 19) first; then choose one of these stitches to make everything safe and secure once again.

Sashiko

Sashiko began as a traditional Japanese mending technique and is still used for overall mending and reinforcing virtually every type of fabric. Be sure to check out the Sashiko chapter (page 80) for marking and stitching details.

STITCH INSTRUCTIONS

The stitches in this section are given in order of most commonly used to less frequently used. In addition, some of these early, foundational stitches are used as the basis for many other stitches, so they are worth learning.

RUNNING STITCH (NON-SASHIKO)

This, along with the backstitch, is the stitch most of us learned when we first started sewing. The running stitching is the go-to stitch for basting, outlining, hemming, attaching patches, and just about every other hand-sewing project. Learn this one and practice it so the movements are second nature for you.

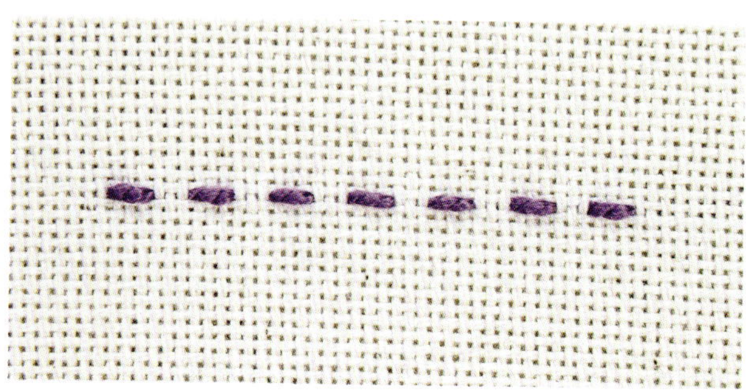

1. Bring your needle up at the start of your stitching line. *fig. A*
2. Insert the needle into the fabric the distance of one stitch. *fig. B*
3. Bring the needle up a stitch length from the first stitch made. *fig. C*
4. Continue to work in this manner, being careful to make your stitches as even (the same length and distance apart) as possible.

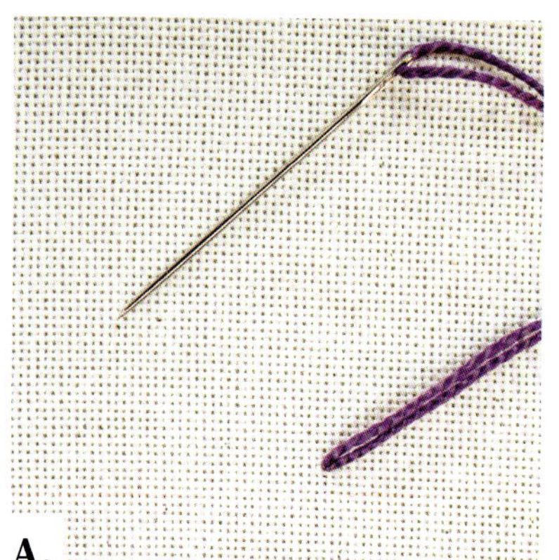

A.

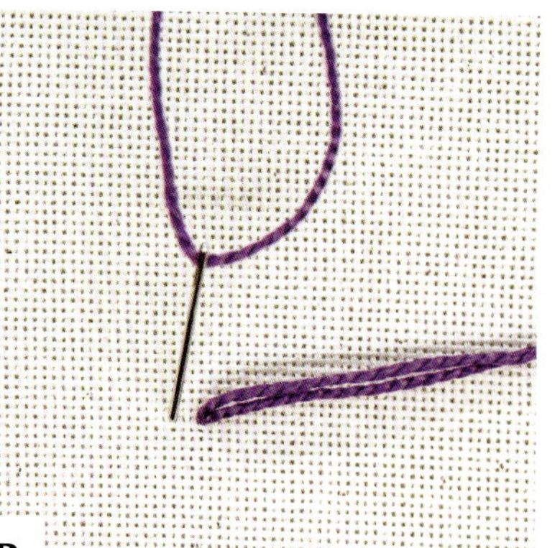

B.

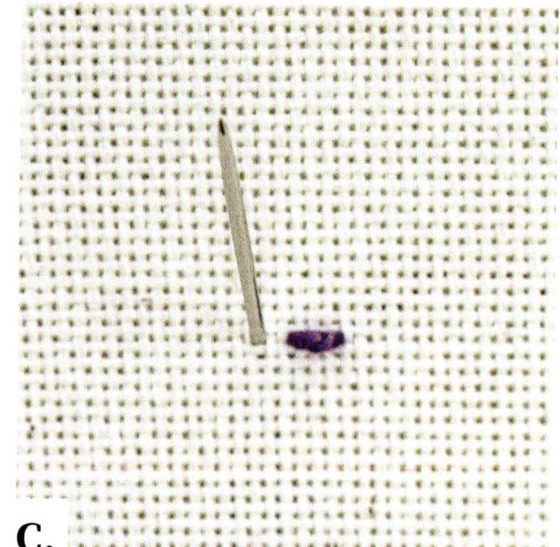

C.

DOUBLE RUNNING STITCH

The double running stitch is an uncomplicated outlining and securing stitch that looks the same on the front and the back of the work. The double running stitch is made in two passes and works equally well for lines or curves.

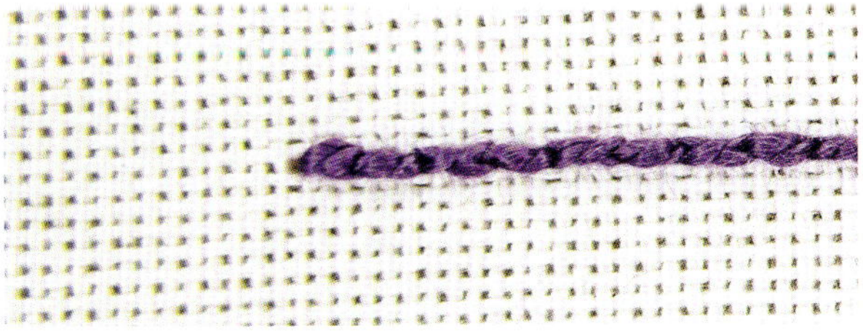

1. Begin the first pass by making a row of running stitches (see Running Stitch [Non-Sashiko], at left). On this first pass, ensure that the stitch length and the space between stitches is the same. *fig. A*

2. At the end of the line of stitching, make the second pass by working running stitches in the opposite direction, coming up through and inserting the needle into the holes at the beginning and end of each stitch of the first pass. *fig. B*

This will create a solid line of stitches that looks the same from the front and the back of the mend.

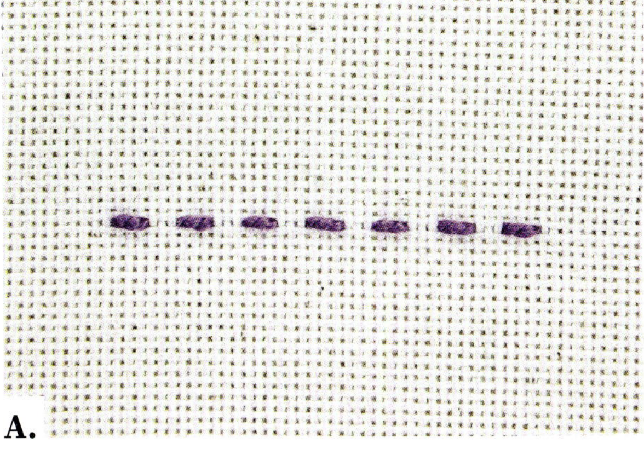

A.

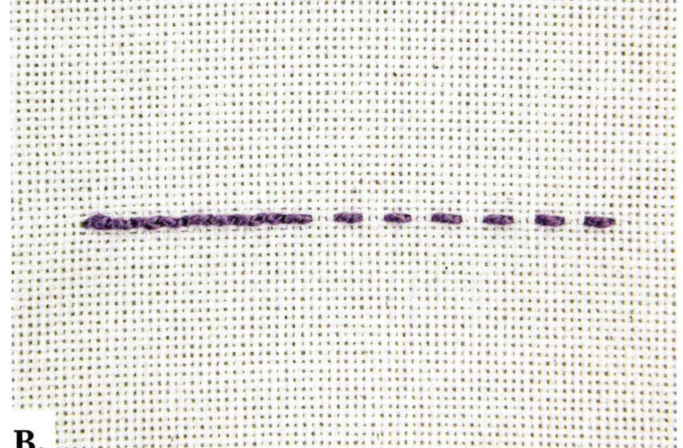

B.

Color Your World

You know we love to mix it up a bit when it comes to color, and the double running stitch is the perfect place to do that. And it's so simple! Use one color for the first pass, and a second color for the second pass. Easy peasy!

BACKSTITCH

Make it straight and true or give it some curves. This is the original outlining stitch and, along with the running stitch, will be the two most used stitches in your mending toolkit. This elemental stitch is ideal for securing patches and making sure edge frays go no further. The backstitch is also the foundation for more decorative stitches, so learn it and practice it so you can whip it out with ease. The backstitch is worked by sliding the needle in and out of the fabric, working back into where the preceding stitch originated.

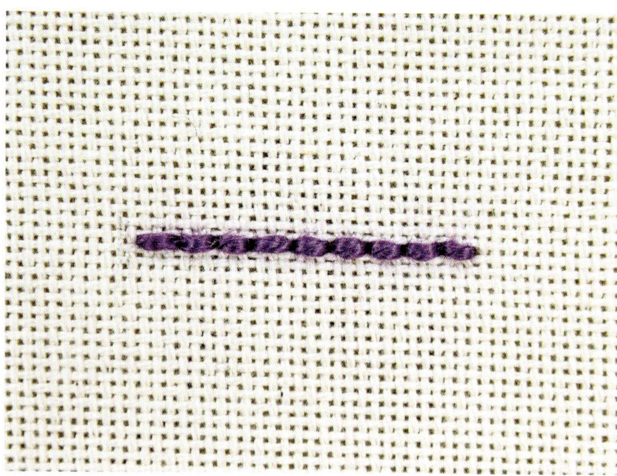

Shorter Is Smarter

When working the backstitch along a tight curve, shorten your stitches to keep the flow of the curve even and consistent.

1. Start by bringing the needle up from back to front, the length of one stitch away from where the line of stitching begins. *fig. A*
2. Insert the needle where the line of stitching begins. *fig. B*

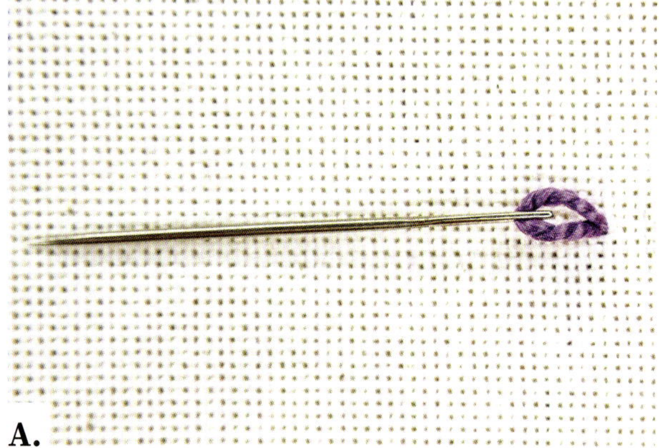

A.

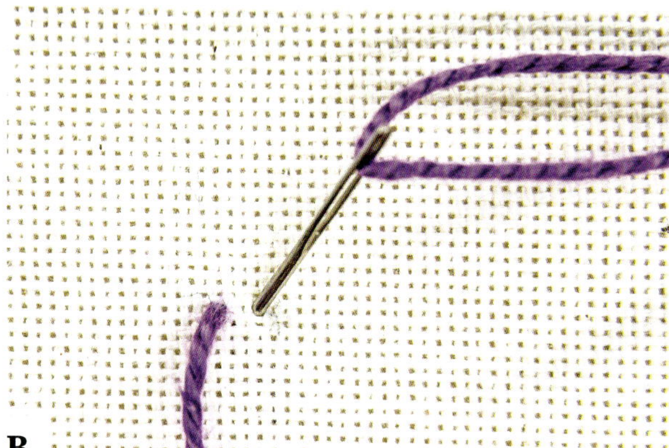

B.

3. Bring the needle back up one stitch length away from the end of the first stitch. *fig. C*
4. Insert the needle in the same hole as in Step 1. *fig. D*
5. Continue making stitches in this manner to the end of the stitching line.

Note: The length of the stitch on the back of the fabric will be twice as long as the stitch on the front of the fabric.

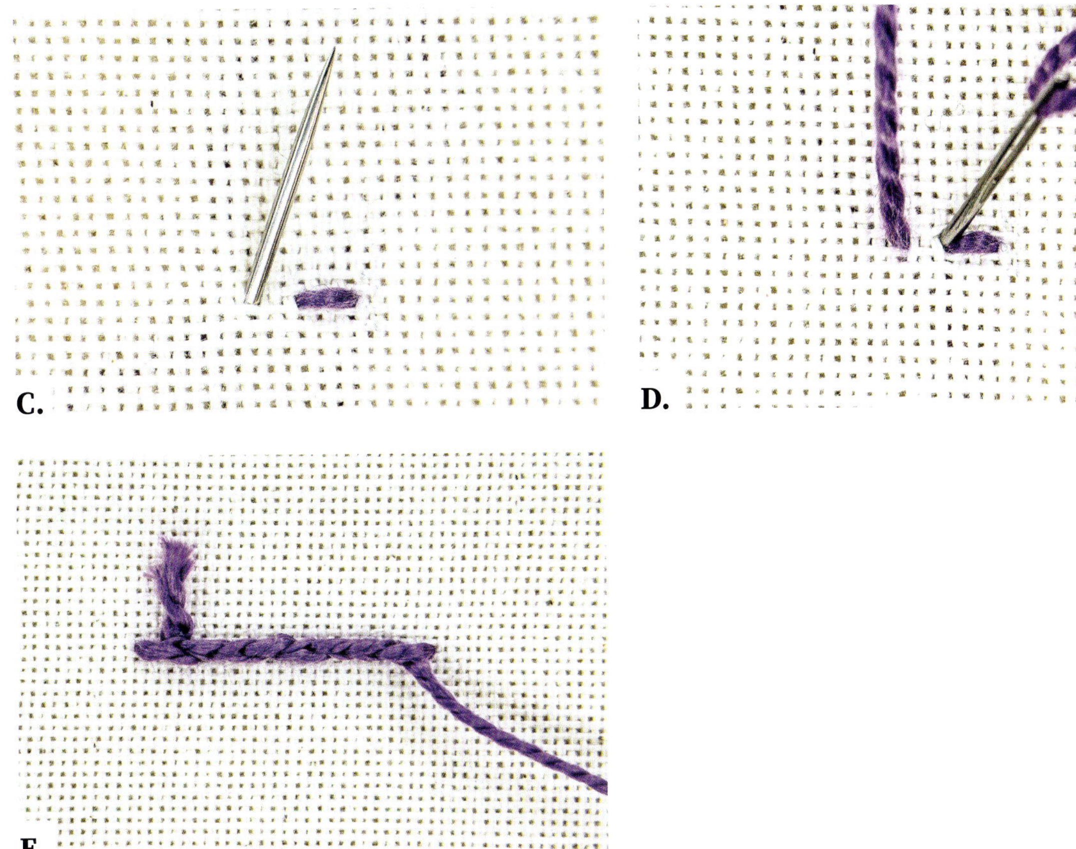

C.

D.

E.

SPLIT STITCH

The split stitch is another elemental stitch that will make your mending stronger and ... well ... look better once you master it. Like the backstitch, the split stitch is ideal for outlining and securing patches.

Fill Your Spaces

Use this stitch with thick thread or yarn for outlining letters or filling spaces.

1. Bring the needle up at the start of the line of stitching. *fig. A*
2. Insert the needle back into the fabric one stitch length away, pulling all of the thread to the back of the fabric. *fig. B*

A.

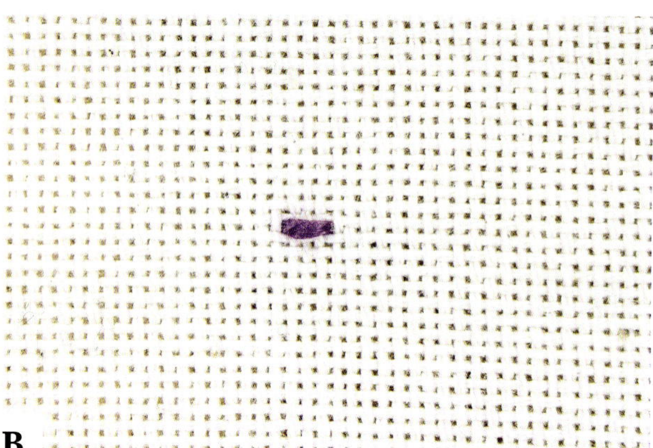

B.

3. Bring the needle up through the fabric at the center point of the first stitch, splitting the first stitch by bringing the needle up through the strands of thread of the first stitch. *fig. C*

4. Insert the needle into the fabric to make a stitch the same length as the first stitch, pulling all of the thread to the back of the fabric as before. *fig. D*

5. Bring the needle back up through the fabric at the center point of the last stitch made and split the thread as before.

6. Continue to make stitches in this manner to the end of the line or shape. *fig. E*

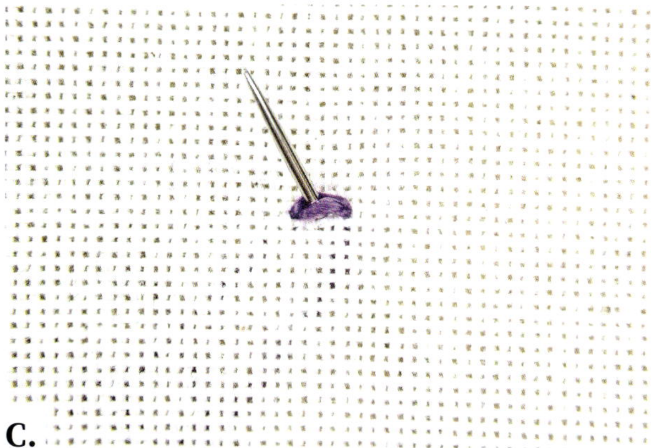

C.

D.

E.

SPLIT BACKSTITCH

The split backstitch is the sibling but not quite twin of the split stitch. Their function for outlining and securing is the same, and they look nearly identical from the front side of the work, but their construction has an essential difference that can make the split backstitch more functional for mending in certain circumstances. The resulting line of solid stitching on both sides of the fabric makes the split backstitch better for decorative work that looks the same from both sides of the mend.

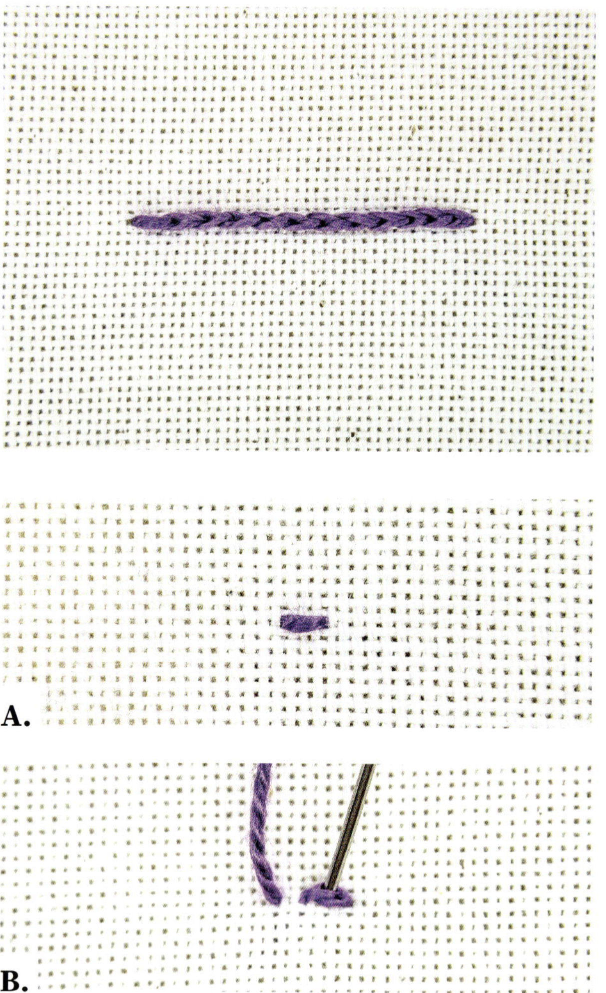

A.

B.

1. Start by making a single backstitch (see Backstitch, page 30). *fig. A*

2. Make a second backstitch, insert the needle from top to bottom, splitting the threads of the first stitch. *fig. B*

3. Continue to make stitches in this way until the line of stitching is finished.

Note • The Flipside

The most significant difference between the split stitch and the split backstitch is on the back of the work. Like a regular backstitch, the split backstitch has a long, connected line of stitches on the back of the work, whereas a split stitch has a broken line of short stitches on the back of the work. This can be significant if there is a concern about snagging stitches on the inside of a mend, in which case the split backstitch would be more appropriate. If a continuous line of stitching that looks the same from the front and the back is desired, the split backstitch is the way to go.

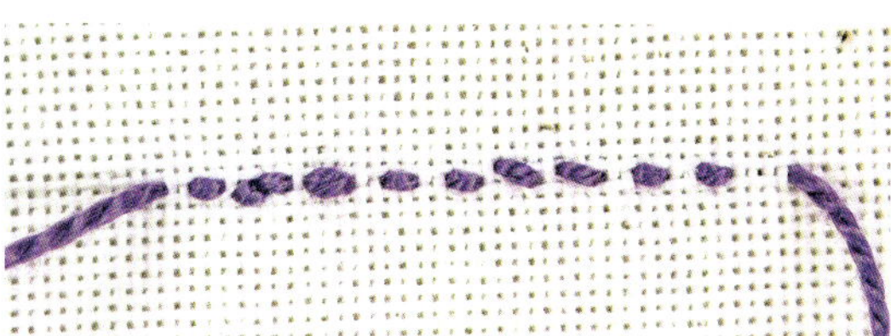

HALF-BACKSTITCH (OPEN BACKSTITCH)

The half-backstitch, sometimes called an open backstitch, is another essential stitch that is perfect for outlining but it is especially effective at locking down the edges of a patch or securing the edges of a mending area. While the half-backstitch and the running stitch look the same from both sides of the mend and they both secure a patch beautifully, the back side of the half-backstitch is a solid line of stitches and is a more secure stitching line. Simple, yet strong and effective.

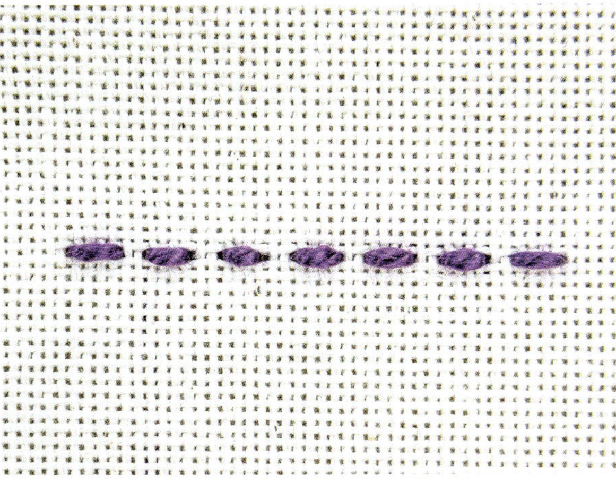

1. Start the line of stitching by making a single backstitch (see Backstitch, page 30). *fig. A*
2. Now move the needle forward on the back side of the fabric the length of the stitch plus the gap between the stitches, and bring the needle up through the fabric. *fig. B*
3. Insert the needle backward against the line of stitching, leaving a gap between the stitch just made. *fig. C*
4. Continue in this manner to the end of the line.

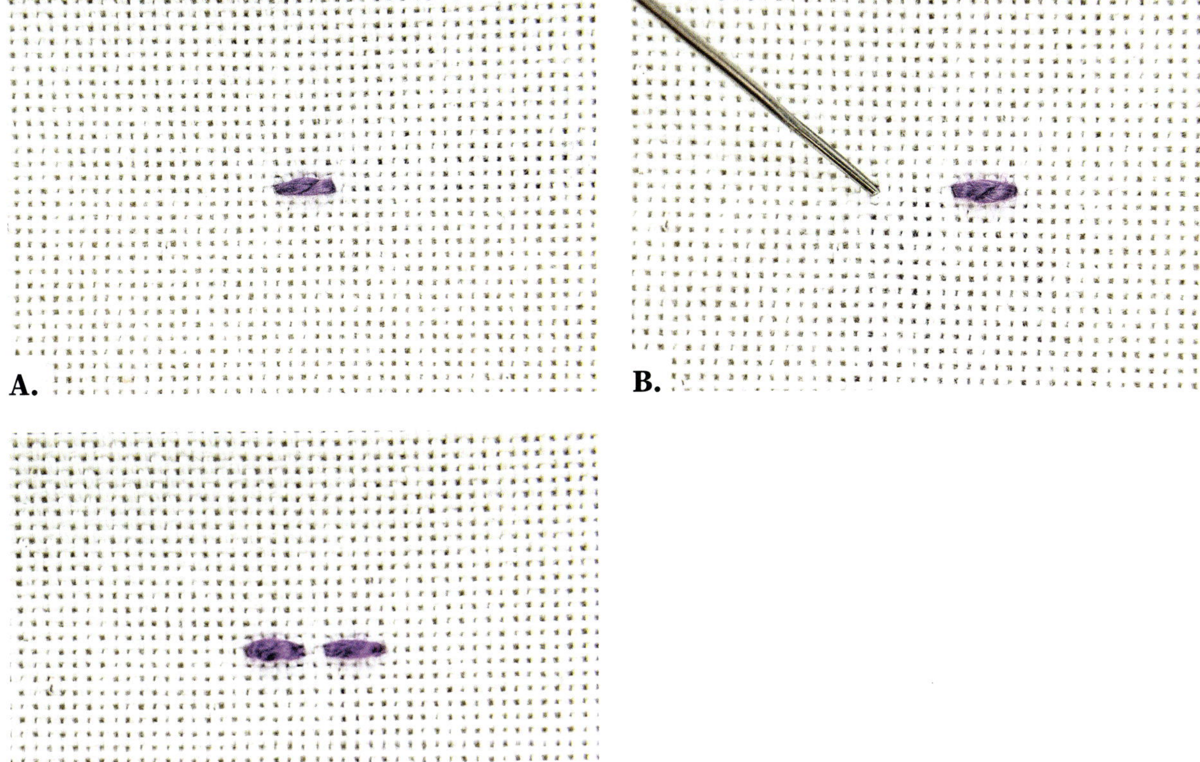

A.

B.

C.

OUTLINE STITCH

Other stitches are good for securing patches, outlining a mending area, or outlining a design element, but this is THE outline stitch. The outline stitch creates a solid line of overlapping stitching that has a decorative twisted look to it and is very secure. The outline stitch is often used interchangeably with the stem stitch, and though they both look very much the same, there are times when one is more appropriate for use than the other (see Opposite Sides of the Same Stitch, page 39).

1. Bring the needle up at the start of the stitching line and make one forward stitch. Leave a loop of the working thread on the top of the stitching line. (A) It is important to hold the thread loop in place to keep it out of the way while making the second part of this stitch. *fig. A*
2. Bring the needle back up halfway between where the stitch starts and ends. Be sure the working loop of thread stays above the needle as it comes through the fabric. *fig. B*

A.

B.

3. Pull the stitch taut, ensuring that the secured loop is now lying above the line of the first stitch. *fig. C*

4. Make another forward stitch and bring the needle back up where the previous stitch ended, again being careful to keep the working thread above the line of stitching. *fig. D*

5. Pull the stitch snug with the now secured loop lying above the line of the stitch just made. *fig. E*

6. Continue making stitches this way to the end of the line.

C.

D.

E.

STEM STITCH

The stem stitch is the mirror image of the outline stitch and is equally good at securing patches, outlining a mending area, or outlining a design element. The difference between the two stitches is where the working loop of thread is laid and held during each succeeding stitch (see Opposite Sides of the Same Stitch, at right).

1. Bring the needle up at the start of the stitching line and make one forward stitch, leaving a loop of the working thread on the bottom of the stitching line. (A) It is important to hold the thread loop in place to keep it out of the way while making the second part of this stitch. *fig. A*
2. Bring the needle back up halfway between where the stitch starts and ends, ensuring that the working loop of thread stays below the needle as it comes through the fabric. *fig. B*
3. Pull the stitch taut, ensuring that the secured loop is now lying below the line of the first stitch. *fig. C*
4. Make another forward stitch and bring the needle back up where the previous stitch ended, again being careful to keep the working thread below the line of stitching. *fig. D*

A.

B.

C.

D.

5. Pull the stitch taut against the surface of the fabric, ensuring that the secured loop is lying below the line of the stitch just made. *fig. E*

6. Continue making stitches this way to the end of the line.

E.

Note • Opposite Sides of the Same Stitch

The outline stitch (page 36) and stem stitch (at left) are nearly identical. They both create a solid line of overlapping stitches with a twisted look that is decorative as well as very secure, BUT... the difference is whether the working loop of thread is held above (outline stitch) or below (stem stitch) the line of stitching. The difference is especially relevant when working curves, as the stitch with the working loop laying on the outside of the curve will create a smoother outside edge, whereas the stitch with the working loop laying on the inside of the curve will leave a small spike. Experiment with both, and mix it up by changing between one and the other to achieve different effects.

Outline stitch

Stem stitch

DARNING STITCH

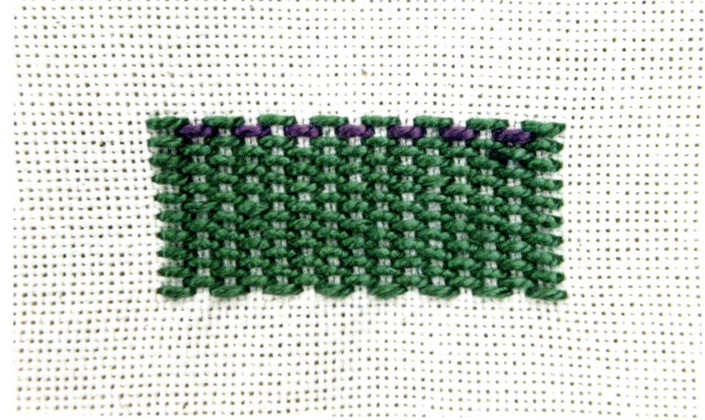

The darning stitch is such a staple of fabric mending that mending cultures from all over the world and as far back as mended fabric fragments have been found contain elements of these closely stacked rows of running stitches. For sashiko folx, the darning stitch will be familiar because it resembles the offset stacked running stitches in both hitomezashi (if the stitches and spaces between the stitches are the same length) and moyouzashi (if the stitches are longer than the spaces). The darning stitch is also the same in concept to kogin-zashi in that it reinforces fabric that is loosely woven or has become threadbare. Whatever your sewing or embroidery background, the darning stitch is the fundamental stitch of the mending world because it is ideal for mending fabric without the use of a patch but is versatile and decorative enough to use for attaching fabric patches to worn, damaged, or stained fabrics.

The length of the stitches, the gap between the stitches, and the distance between the rows of stitches will depend on how dense the base fabric is that needs mending. Fabric that is more threadbare or loosely woven will require shorter stitches and very little space between the stitches to reinforce and mend the fabric. In some cases, stabilizer may be needed to further reinforce a mend.

When outlining the area to be mended, allow for an additional space of about 1″–2″ (2.5–5cm) on all sides of the mended area. This will ensure that the mend is completely covered and the surrounding fabric cannot succumb to damage.

1. Start by making a row of running stitches (see Running Stitch, page 28). *fig. A*

2. Turn the work and make another row of running stitches that stacks like bricks across the gaps of the previous row. *fig. B*

3. Continue making rows of stacked running stitches until the mend is covered.

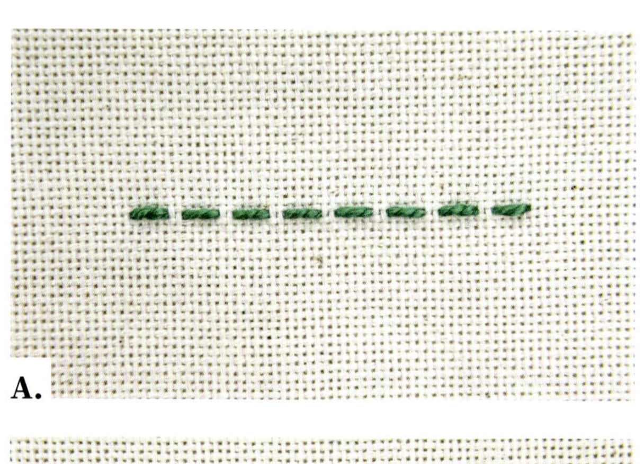

A.

B.

Better Than Before

If you are going to mend an area of fabric that can be seen, don't be afraid to turn it into a feature. Instead of a simple square or rectangle, mark the outline of the area to be mended with a heart or a triangle or a silhouette representing a hobby or sportsing thingamabob. If you are going to take the time to make a mend, make it better than it was before!

Add a Little Creative Chaos!

If the mend is on fabric that has a little stretch to it (like stretch denim) or you just really do NOT trust that it is going to be reinforced by one pass of darning stitches, don't be afraid to make an area of crisscrossing darning stitches. We like the resulting chaotic stitches that mesh and fly apart in all directions, and there is no way this mending is giving way any time soon.

DOUBLE DARNING STITCH

The double darning stitch consists of rows of double running stitches (see Darning Stitch, at left) stacked on top of one another to fill the mend area. As simple as that sounds, it is a very effective reinforcing stitch for woven and knit fabrics and securely holds patches in place.

JAPANESE DARNING STITCH

The Japanese darning stitch is another of those decorative embroidery stitch patterns that translates directly to mending with great effect. The use of brick-like stacks of offset running stitches combined with leaning stitches that lace the rows together makes this a secure stitch for holding patches in place and a great alternative for other stack-and-block-style stitches. A guide grid drawn on the mending areas is helpful to ensure stitches are evenly spaced.

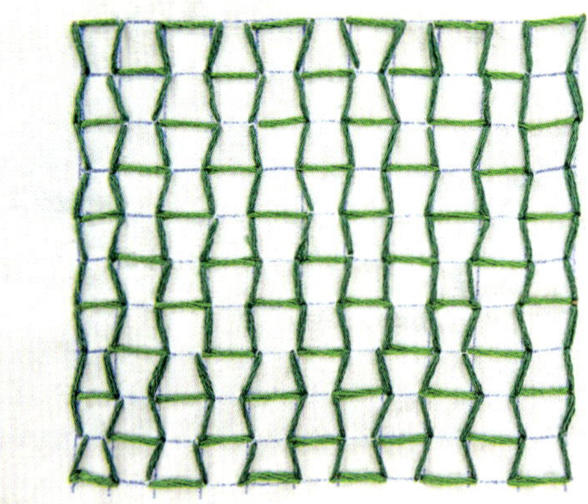

1. Work a series of rows of offset running stitches (see Running Stitch, page 28), with the space between the stitches slightly shorter than the stitches themselves. *fig. A*

2. Bring the needle up at the end of the first stitch of the row (A) and insert it into the end of the offset stitch of the row below (B). This creates a diagonal-leaning stitch. *fig. B*

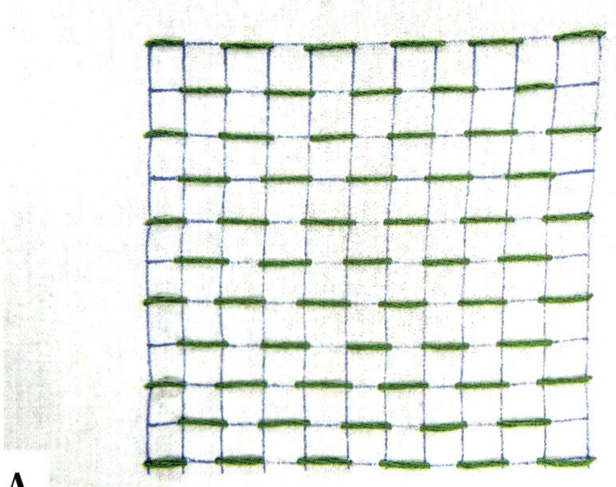

A.

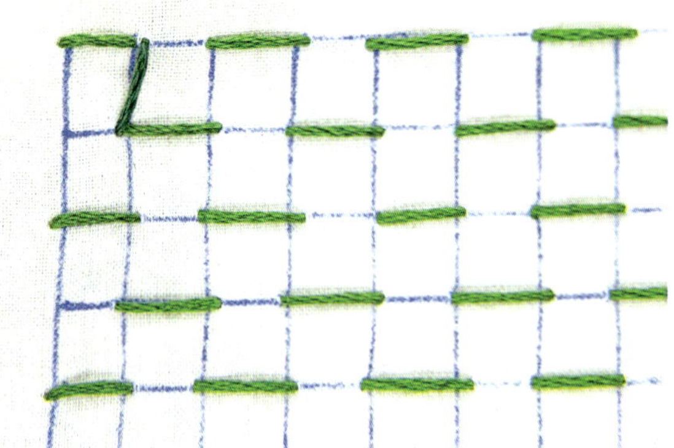

B.

3. Bring the needle up at the end of the same stitch. *fig. C*

4. Insert the needle into the end of the next offset stitch of the row above (D) to create another diagonal leaning stitch. *fig. D*

5. Continue to work from the ends of stitches of one row to the ends of the offset stitch in the neighboring row to the end of the row. *fig. E*

6. To work multiple rows of the Japanese darning stitch, continue with the next row by connecting the ends of those running stitches with diagonal stitches to the previously worked row. *fig. F*

7. Continue to connect as many additional rows as needed to cover the mend.

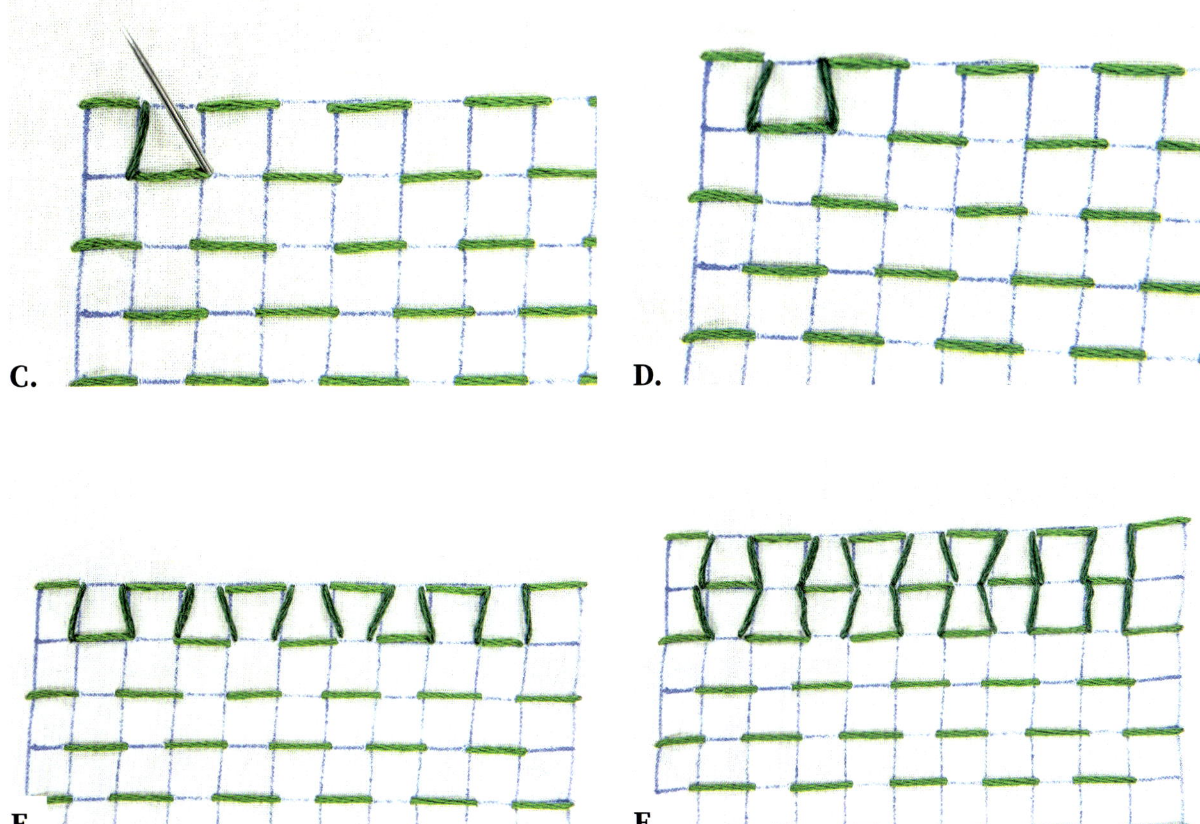

CHAIN STITCH

The chain stitch is perfect for outlines, borders, curved patterns, and shapes, and for filling designs. For a clean chain, use the same hole to come up and go back down. Be careful to not overtighten.

1. Bring the needle up at the beginning of the stitching line. *fig. A*
2. Make a loop with the working thread, and hold the loop toward the line of stitching. *fig. B*
3. Insert the needle back into the same hole (A) the needle came out of. *fig. C*
4. Bring the needle up a short distance along the line of stitching and through the loop. *fig. D*

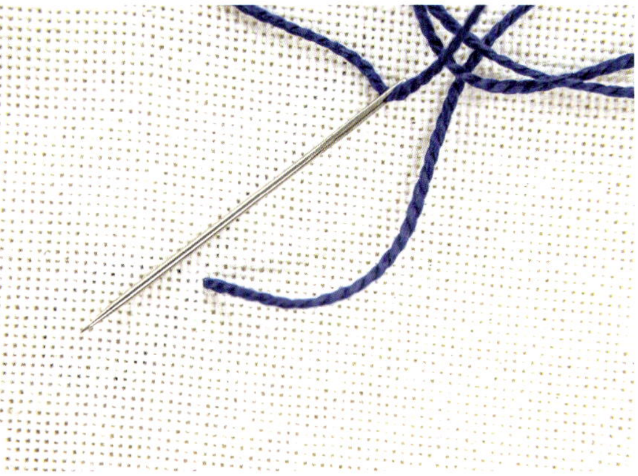

A.

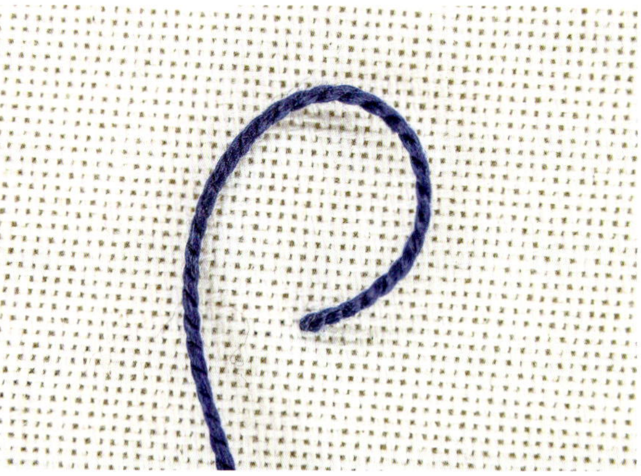

B.

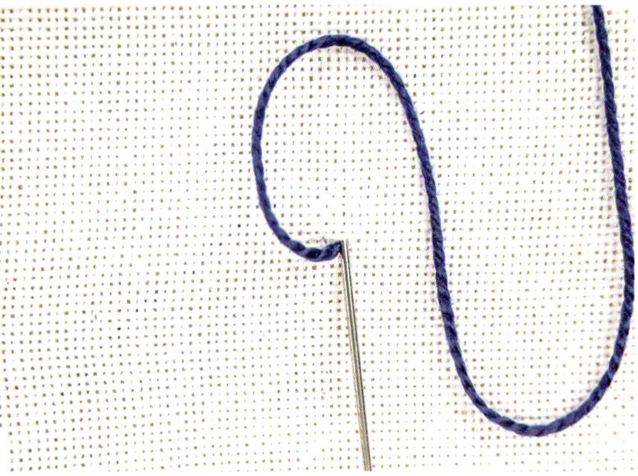

C.

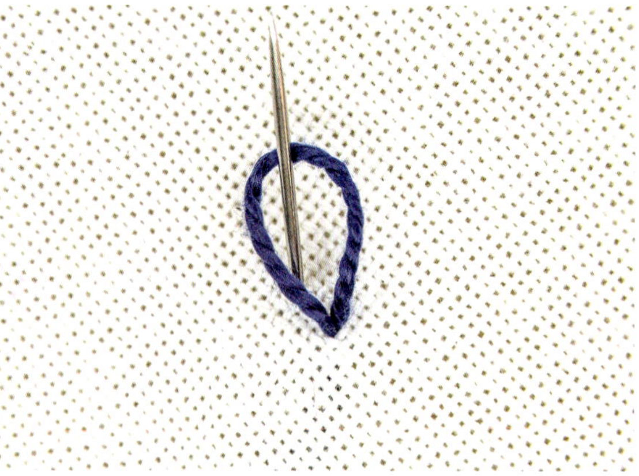

D.

5. Pull the loop snug but not too tight. First chain made. *fig. E*

6. While holding the working thread in a loop, insert the needle back into the hole it just came out of *fig. F*

7. Bring the needle up the same distance as the last stitch made, passing the needle through the loop. *fig. G*

8. Pull the stitch to gently tighten the loop. *fig. H*

9. To end the line of chain stitch, make one small stitch over the end of the last loop.

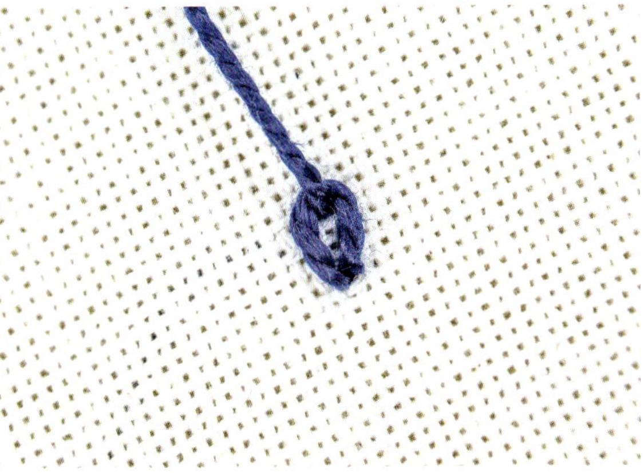

E.

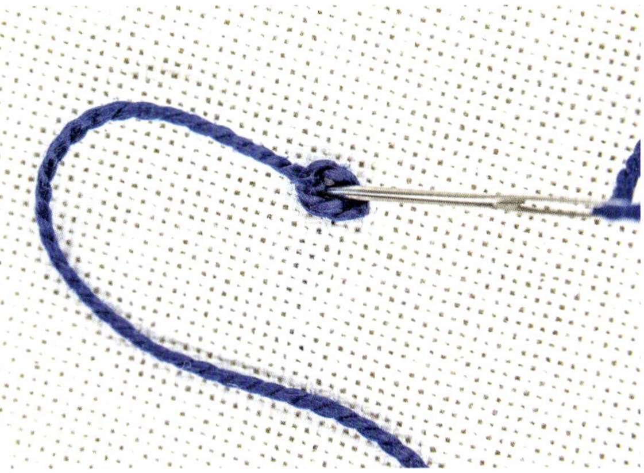

F.

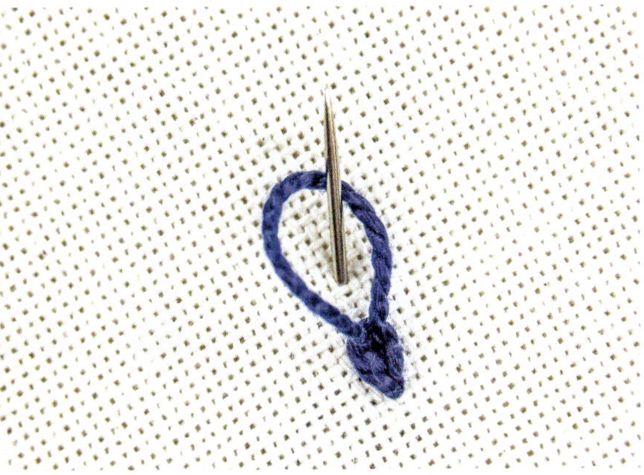

G.

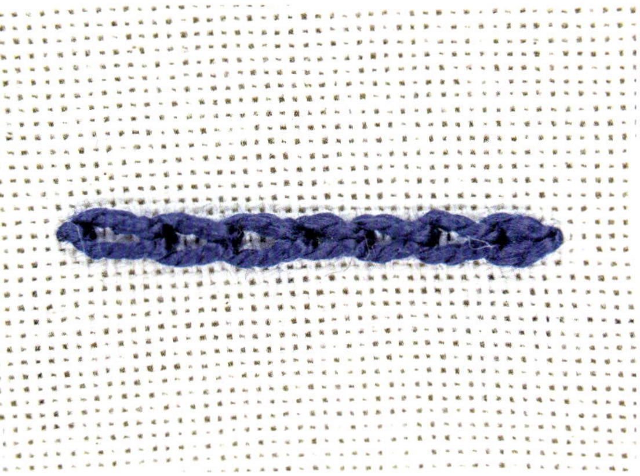

H.

Chain Stitch in a Circle

1. To finish a seamless circular line of chain stitches, pass the needle under the two sides of the loop of the first chain stitch made. *fig. A*

2. Insert the needle back into the hole it just came out of and pull snug.

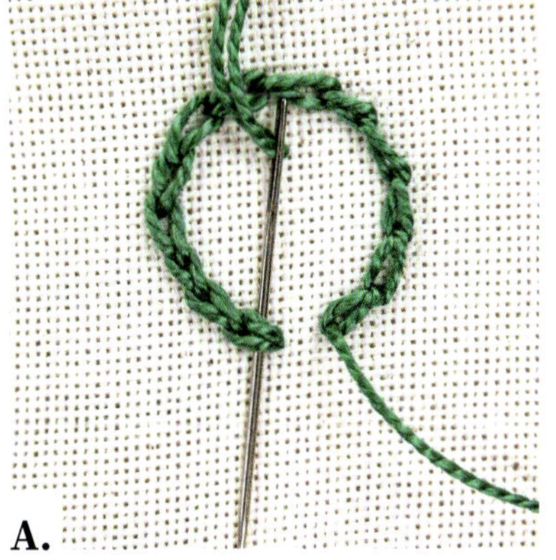

A.

REVERSE CHAIN STITCH

The reverse chain stitch looks identical to the regular chain stitch. The difference? It is created backward ... in reverse ... get it?

1. Start by making an anchor stitch by bringing the needle up at the start of the stitching line (A) and back into the fabric a very short distance away along thc line of stitching (B). *fig. A*
2. Bring the needle up along the line of stitching the desired length of the chain stitch (C). *fig. B*
3. Pass the needle under the anchor stitch. *fig. C*
4. Insert the needle back into the hole it just came out of (C). First chain made. *fig. D*

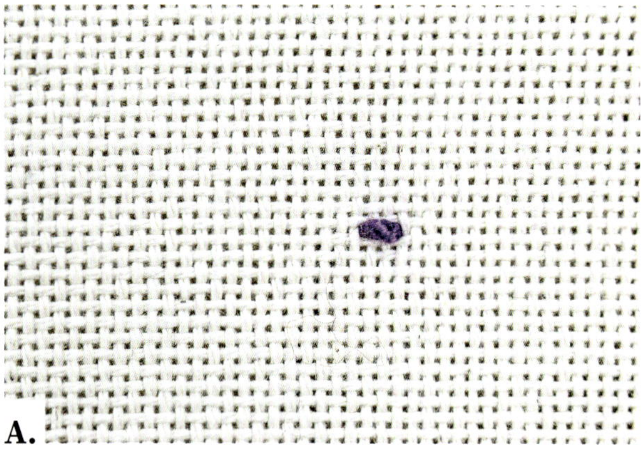

A.

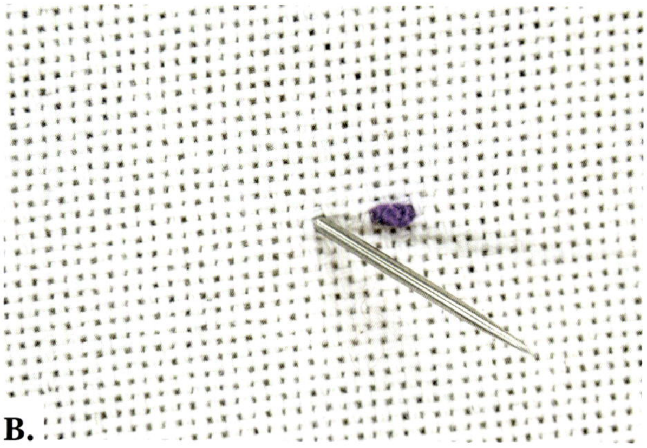

B.

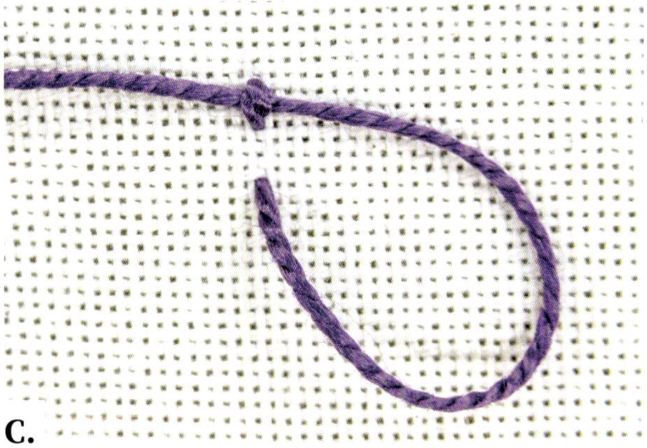

C.

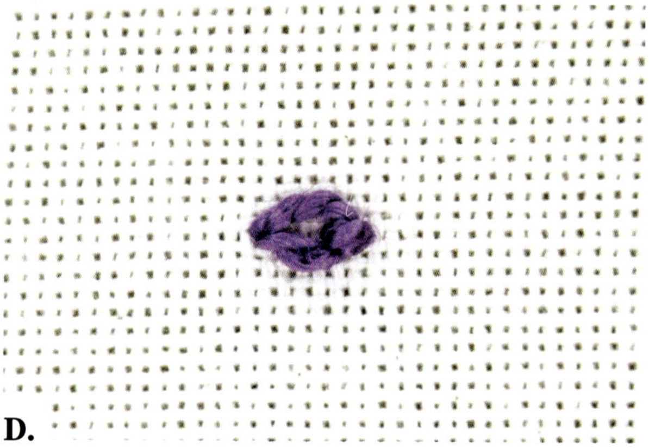

D.

5. Bring the needle up again along the line of stitching (D) the distance of one chain stitch. *fig. E*

6. Pass the needle under both sides of the loop of the chain stitch just made. *fig. F*

7. Insert the needle back into the hole it just came out of (D). Next chain stitch made. *fig. G*

8. Continue making reverse chain stitches in this manner to the end of the stitching line or shape.

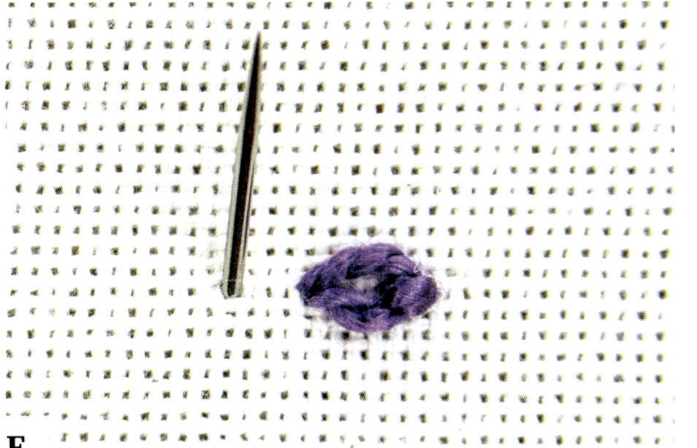

E.

F.

G.

Reverse Chain in a Circle

1. To finish a seamless circular line of reverse chain stitches, bring the needle up inside the first reverse chain stitch made (A).

2. Pass the needle under both sides of the loop of the last reverse chain stitch made. *fig. A*

3. Insert the needle back into the same hole it just came out of (A). *fig. B*

A.

B.

Note • By Any Other Name

The slip stitch and the ladder stitch are often presented as interchangeable and even as the same stitch with different names. Further, both are called the invisible or disappearing stitches. We both learned them as separate stitches and present them here as such. The difference is the length the needle travels once it enters the fabric before it exits the fabric making one complete stitch. In the slip stitch, the needle picks up only a few threads from both pieces of fabric; in the ladder stitch, a tiny stitch (a "bite") is taken out of one side of the fabric with a longer stitch taken on the other side. These tiny "bite" stitches are nearly invisible on the surface of the fabric and are the reason for both being called invisible or disappearing. Why one versus the other? Security of the finished stitching (a mend for our purposes here).

SLIP STITCH

The slip stitch is a tool primarily utilized for sewing together the openings of turned fabric projects like coasters and pillows, but it is also excellent for turned-edge appliqué; sewing on patches; and fixing hems, cuffs, and collars. This is because the stitch utilizes small stitches, taking a "bite" of only two or three threads from the fabric. The result is a nearly invisible stitch from both sides of the fabric.

1. Start by bringing the needle up through the fold of the fabric (or behind the fabric if there is no fold) to hide the knot. *fig. A*

2. Insert the needle into the top of the fabric directly across from where the needle exited the first stitch and pick up 2 or 3 threads with the tip of the needle. *fig. B*

3. Insert the needle into the fabric directly across from where the needle exited the stitch just made and pick up 2 or 3 threads to make a stitch. *fig. C*

4. Continue to take small "bites" of fabric from each side of the fabric until the mend is complete.

A.

B.

C.

LADDER STITCH

The ladder stitch is another one of the staples of hand sewing that translates perfectly to mending for securing turned edges and finished edge patches as well as fixing hems and cuffs. The ladder stitch utilizes a sewing motion and a combination of small "bite" stitches and longer running stitches.

1. Start by bringing the needle up through the fold of the fabric (or below the fabric if there is no fold) to hide the knot. *fig. A*

2. For the first stitch, use the needle to take a small "bite" of fabric from the opposite side of the seam—the front side of the fabric. *fig. B*

3. Now insert the needle back into the folded fabric directly across from where the last stitch was completed, slide the needle a short way down the fold, and complete the stitch. *fig. C*

4. Insert the needle into the fabric directly across from where the needle exited the longer stitch just made and pick up 2 or 3 threads to make a stitch.

Continue to take small "bites" of fabric from each side of the fabric until the mend is complete.

A.

B.

C.

BLIND HEM STITCH

The blind hem stitch is similar to the slip stitch with tiny "bites" taken out of both sides of the fabric making it almost completely invisible. The difference is that the stitches are made diagonally to one another, and one side of the fabric is folded against the main fabric. With a little practice, this is the ideal quick hem stitch.

1. Start by bringing the needle up through the back of the fabric to hide the knot. *figs. A-B*

2. For the first stitch, use a sewing motion to insert the needle into the main fabric under just a few threads and pull the thread snug. *fig. C*

3. Now use the same sewing motion and insert the needle into the folded fabric under just a few threads diagonally from the stitch just made. *fig. D*

4. With the same motion, move the needle forward diagonally from the stitch just made and take a small "bite" of fabric from the main fabric. *fig. E*

5. Continue to use a sewing motion and advancing the needle diagonally relative to the stitch just made, alternating between the folded fabric and the main fabric.

A.  **B.**

C.  **D.**  **E.**

HERRINGBONE STITCH (CATCH STITCH)

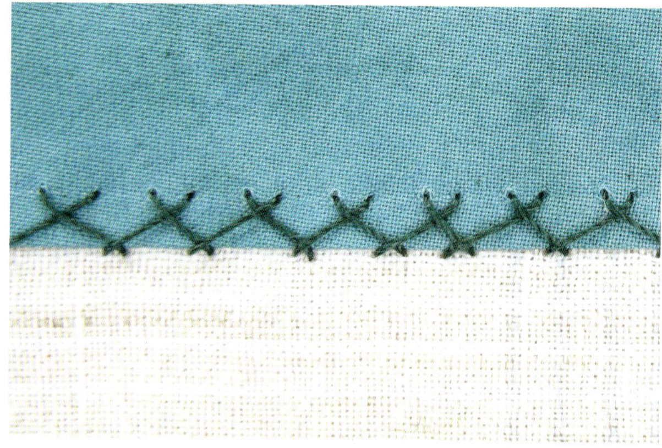

The herringbone stitch (also known as the catch stitch) straddles the line between decorative and functional stitching. It is great for securing a ripped out hem, securing a patch, or decorating the edges of a mend. The herringbone stitch is made using backstitches placed diagonally from one another along the line of stitching. The only difference between a catch stitch and a herringbone stitch is the size of the small "bite" stitch. The idea of a catch stitch is to hold a hem in place with the longer stitches hidden on the inside of the fabric with the small "bite" stitch being so small that it barely shows on the outside of the fabric.

1. Bring the needle up through both layers of fabric or the base fabric and the patch. *fig. A*
2. Make a backstitch into the base fabric diagonally from where the needle came up. *fig. B*
3. Moving diagonally, make a backstitch in line with where the needle came up initially. *fig. C*
4. The working line of thread should cross the diagonal line of thread created by the last stitch made. *fig. D*
5. Repeat this sequence of diagonally placed backstitches until the patch is fully secured.

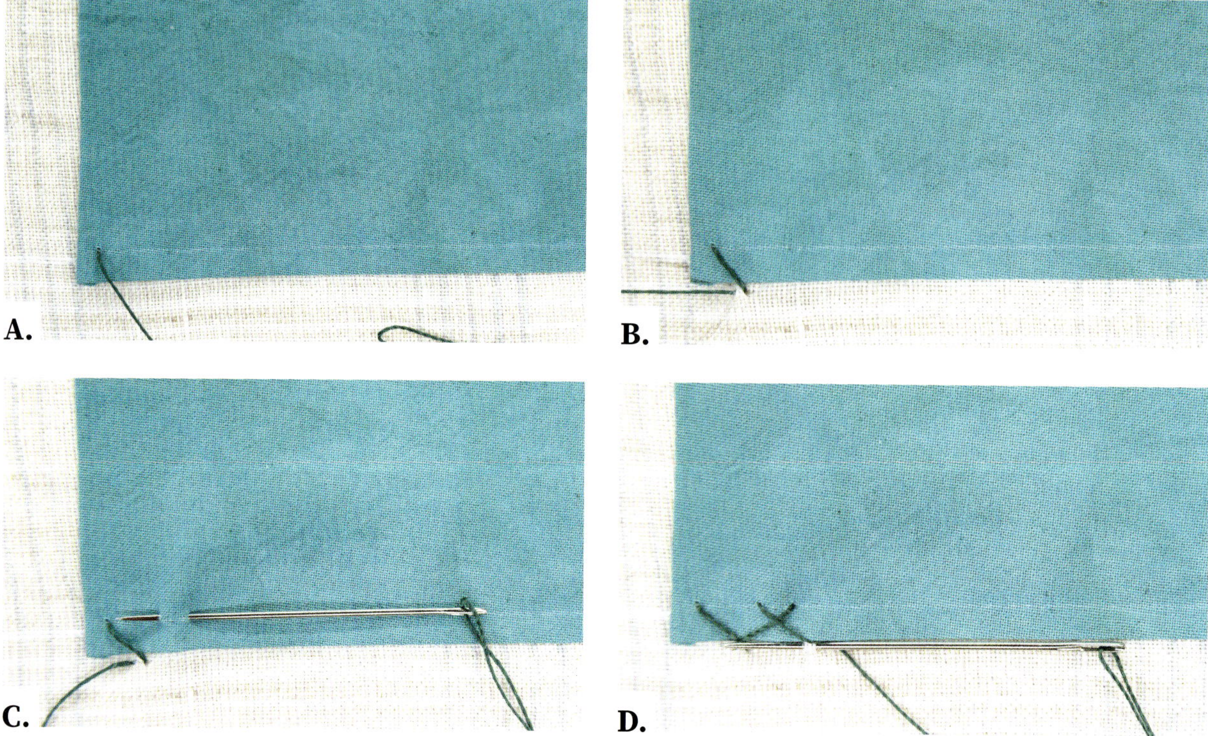

DOUBLE HERRINGBONE STITCH

Simply two layers of herringbone (at left), with a second row placed in the blank section of the first pass. Try it with alternating colors!

WHIPSTITCH

This unassuming stitch is the versatile go-to of sewing, mending, and embroidery. The whipstitch joins together two pieces of fabric, locks down the edges of a patch, holds the edges of a hole in place to prevent further fraying or tearing, and is a must for design elements like couching to enhance your mends. The whipstitch creates a line of diagonal stitches that lean toward the direction of stitching.

1. Bring the needle up from back to front. *fig. A*
2. Insert the needle above and diagonally forward along the direction of stitching.This will make a diagonal stitch leaning toward the direction of stitching. *fig. B*
3. Bring the needle back to the front of the fabric directly below where the needle was inserted and in line with where the needle came out of the fabric at the beginning of the first stitch. *fig. C*
4. Continue making diagonal stitches to the end of the line.

A.

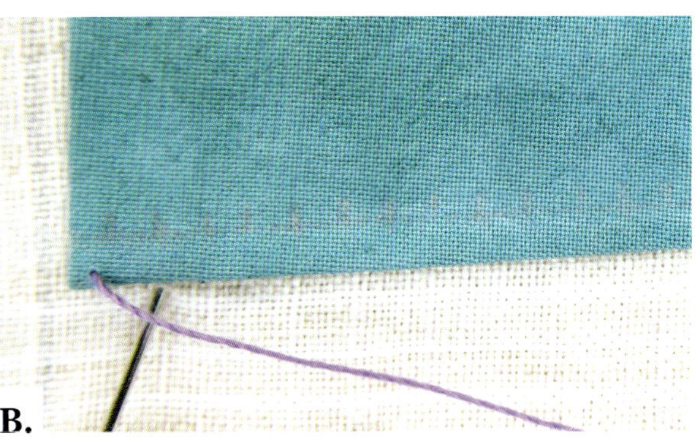

B.

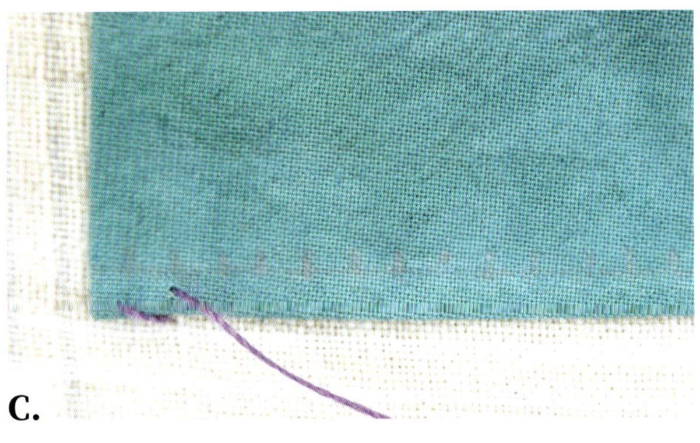

C.

Mark It Up

As we said in Prep the Mend (page 16), marking lines will ensure that your stitches move along an even line. For stitches like the whipstitch, it is also helpful to add additional marks along the guidelines to keep stitches evenly spaced.

APPLIQUÉ STITCH

The appliqué stitch is nearly invisible and creates horizontal rows of stitches, whereas the whipstitch creates diagonal rows of stitches. *This is the perfect stitch for sewing on patches.* With the appliqué stitch, the needle is held at a diagonal using the sewing method to come out of the fabric layers diagonally to where the needle was inserted.

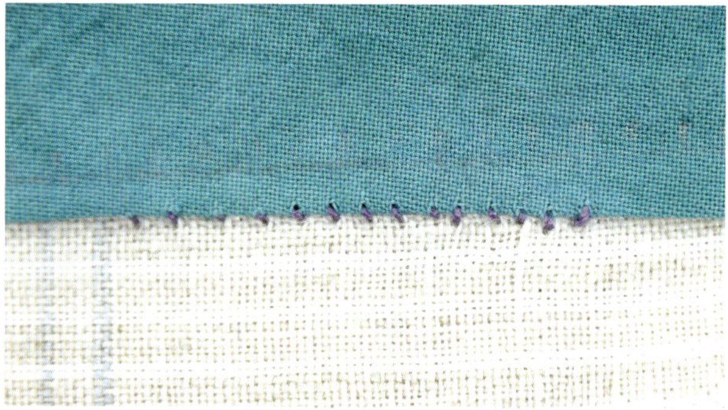

1. Insert the needle with knotted thread into the fold of the appliqué patch fabric or into the back of the patch if the edge is finished. *fig. A*
2. Holding the needle at a diagonal, insert the needle into the base layer of fabric directly across from where the needle came out of the top fabric and bring the needle out of the top fabric one stitch length away from the last finished stitch (C). *fig. B*
3. Continue in this manner until the patch is secured.

A.

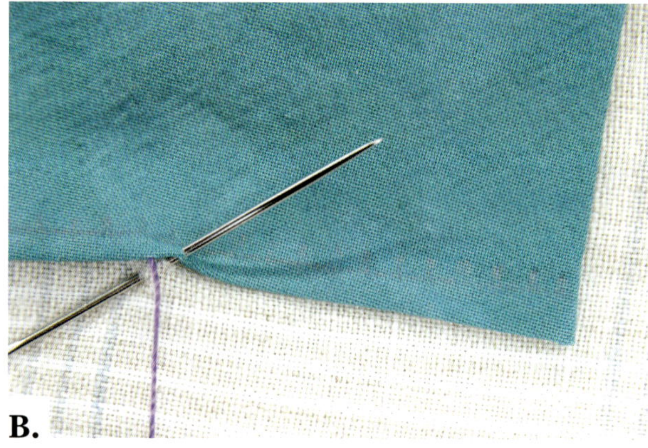

B.

BLANKET STITCH

The blanket stitch is a staple for embroidering, quilting, and, of course, mending! Use this versatile stitch for outlining, for affixing patches, and for securing the raw edges of fabric.

Blanket Stitch for Edges

It will be helpful to mark a line along the edge of the fabric, as well as marks along that line to keep stitches the same height and evenly spaced. *fig. A*

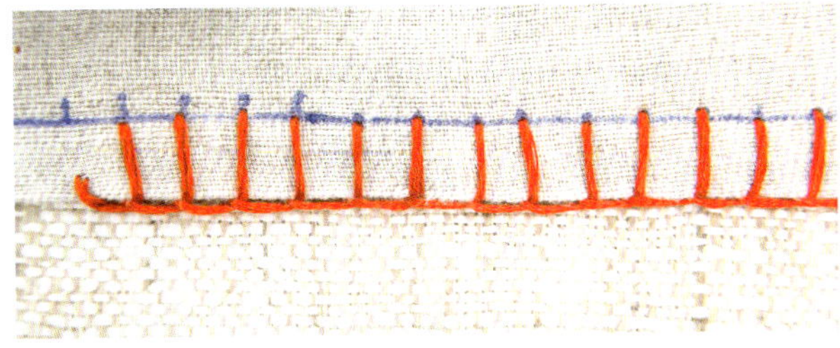

Start by making an anchor stitch at one end of the edge to be stitched.

1. Bring the needle up a little ways in from the edge of the fabric. *fig. B*
2. Wrap the thread over the edge and back up through the same spot. Do not tighten the loop until the next step. *fig. C*
3. Pass the needle through the loop just made before tightening. Anchor stitch made. *fig. D*

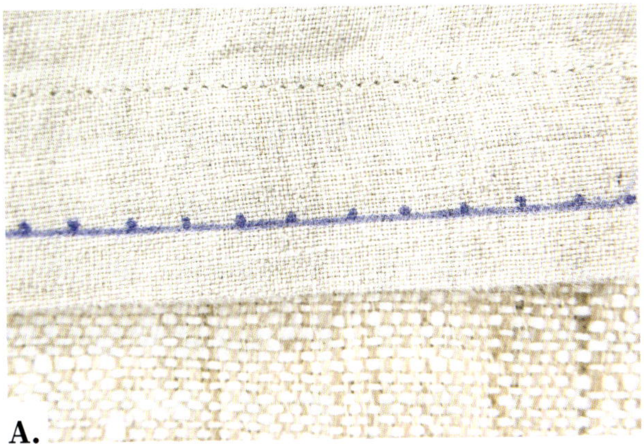

A.

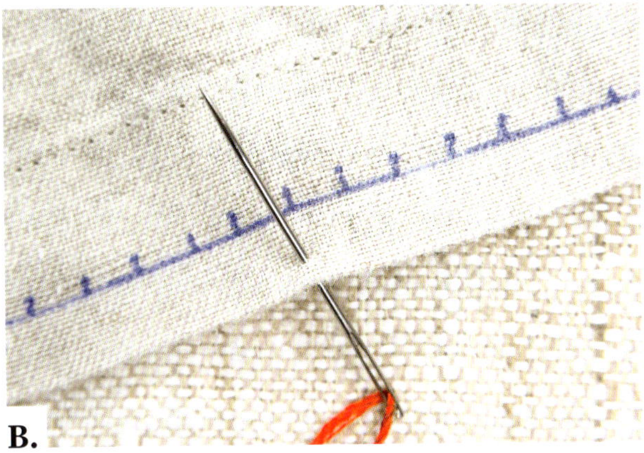

B.

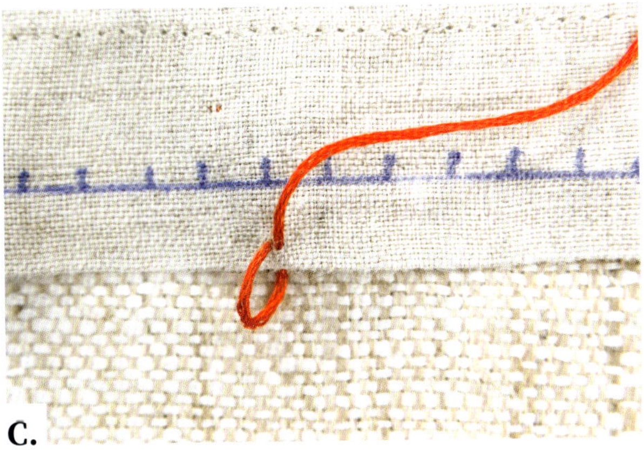

C.

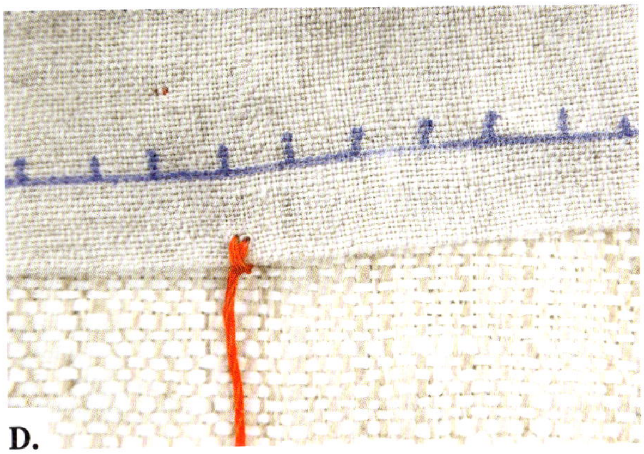

D.

4. Hold the working thread in the direction of stitching to create a loop. Moving along the line of stitching, insert the needle from front to back and bring the needle up directly below where the needle was inserted and through the loop. *fig. E*

5. Pull the thread through the loop and gently tighten, being careful not to pucker the edge of the fabric. *fig. F*

6. Continue working in this manner to the end of the line of stitching or the edge of the fabric.

To end a line of blanket stitch, make a tack stitch by repeating the steps of an anchor stitch from the beginning of the stitch.

If there is a corner to the fabric, make three stitches around the corner in one hole. *fig. G*

To work all the way around a piece of fabric, end the last stitch by passing the needle over the first edge loop and the active loop. *fig. H*

Tighten the edge stitch as before. *fig. I*

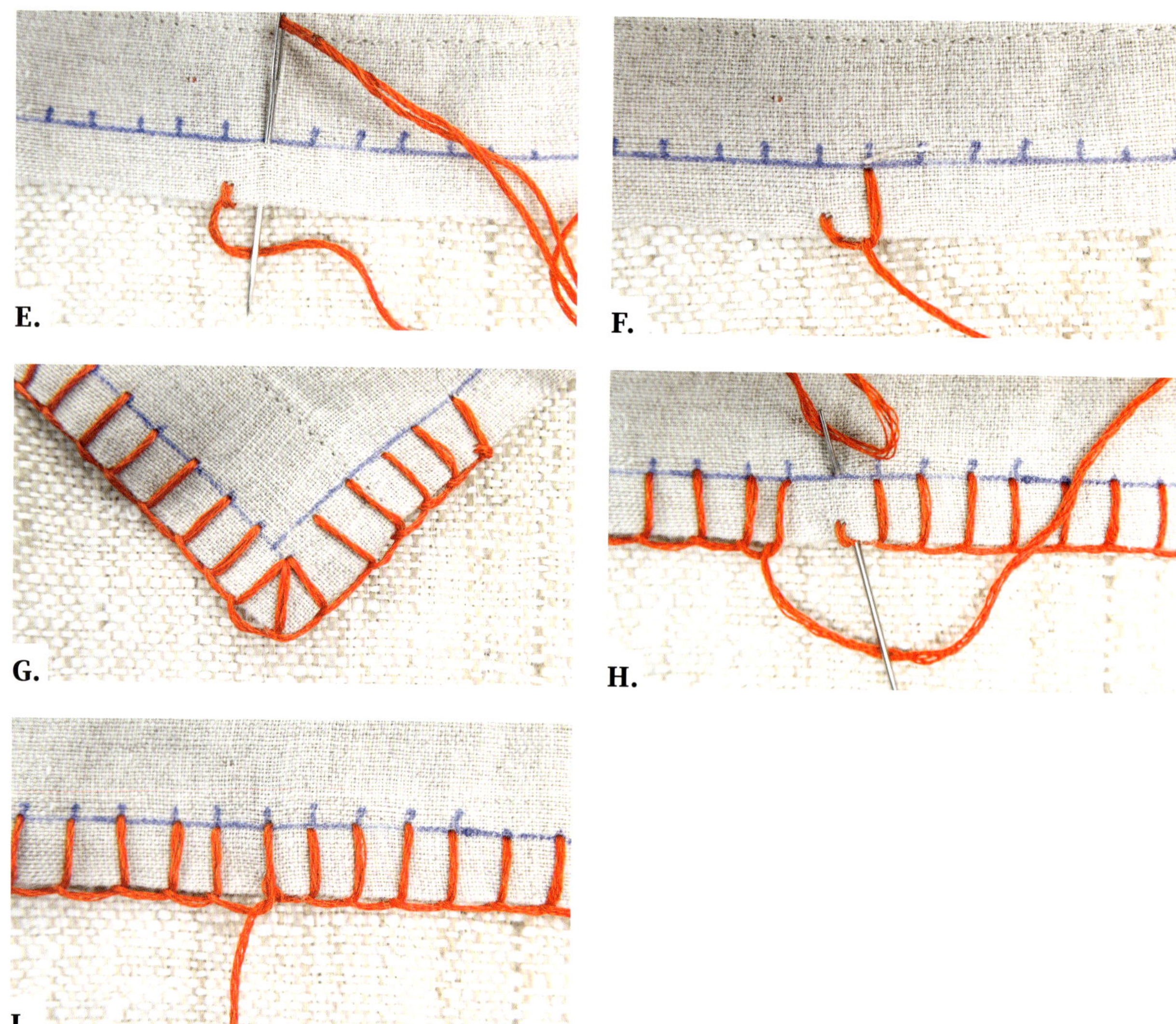

E.

F.

G.

H.

I.

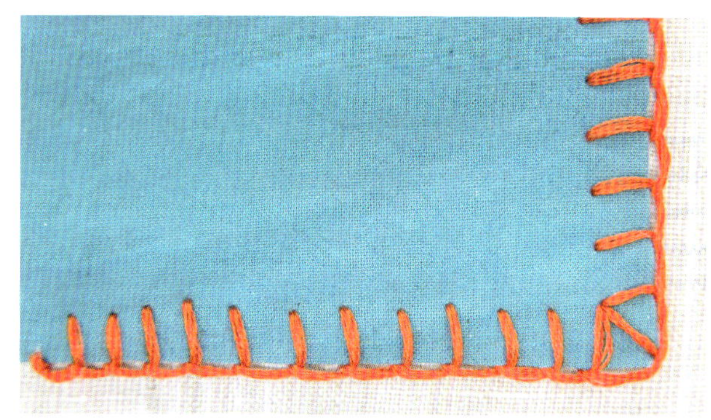

Blanket Stitch for Appliqué

1. Make an anchor stitch by bringing the needle up through the main fabric and the patch close to the edge of the patch. *fig. A*

2. Insert the needle into the main fabric close to the edge of the patch. *fig. B*

3. Bring the needle back up through the same hole in the patch creating a loop. Do not tighten this loop until the next step. *fig. C*

4. Pass the needle under this loop along the edge of the patch and tighten the loop. Anchor stitch made. *fig. D*

5. Hold the working thread in the direction of stitching to create a loop. Moving along the line of stitching, insert the needle into the patch and main fabric from front to back and bring the needle up at the edge of the patch directly below where the needle was inserted passing through the loop. *fig. E*

6. Gently tighten the loop. *fig. F*

7. Continue stitching in this manner along the edge of the patch.

To turn corners and finish the end of the line of stitching, see Blanket Stitch (page 55).

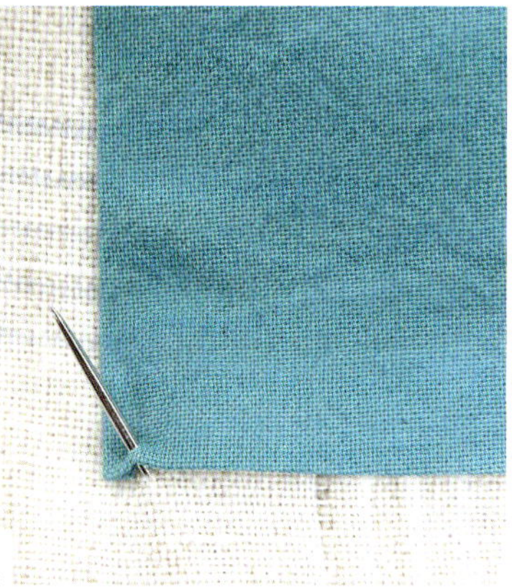

A.

B.

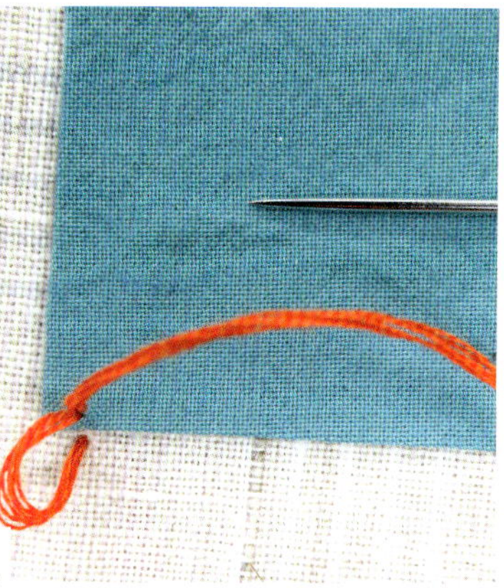

C.

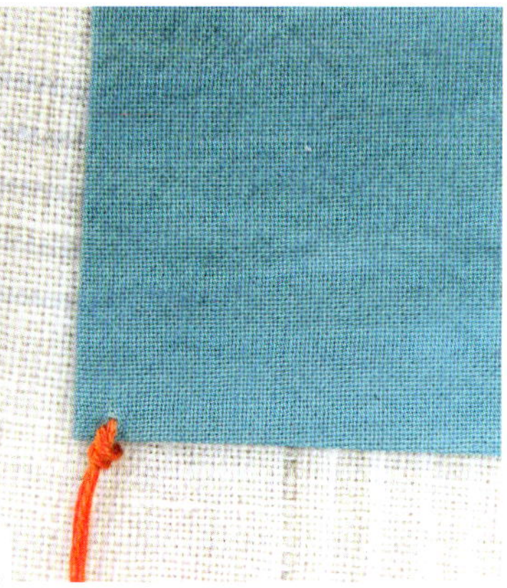

D.

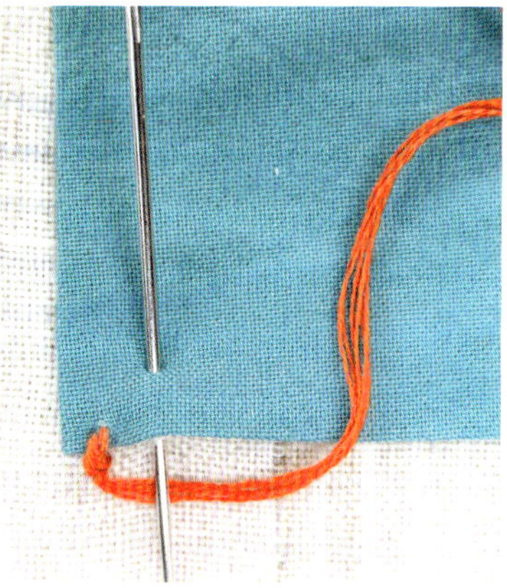

E.

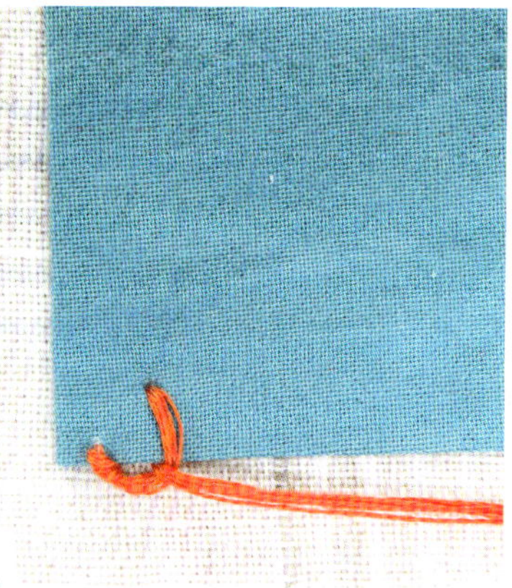

F.

DOUBLE BLANKET STITCH

Simply put, the double blanket stitch is a blanket stitch worked in two rows where the legs of the stitch intermingle with the blank spaces of the opposite row, making a decorative keystone border. Use this variation for extra oomph on borders and patches.

BLANKET STITCH SUNBURST

We love this variation on the blanket stitch (page 55) for securing the edges of holes or for attaching small circular patches. A series of these scattered over an area to be mended secures and strengthens the overall fabric. Plus it looks good. Just sayin'.

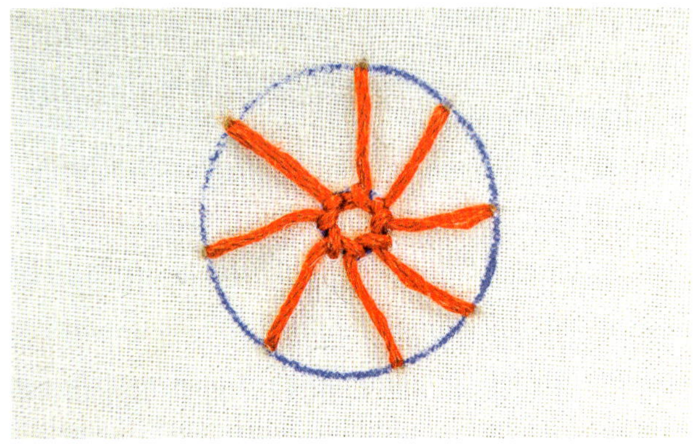

For practice, it is helpful to mark two roundish shapes, one inside the other, as shown in the diagram below.

The key to making this stitch look good is to keep the stitches on the inside of the shape small while fanning out the legs around the outside of the shape to create the sunburst or flower effect. *fig. A*

1. Start by bringing the needle up at (A) on the inside circle. *fig. B*

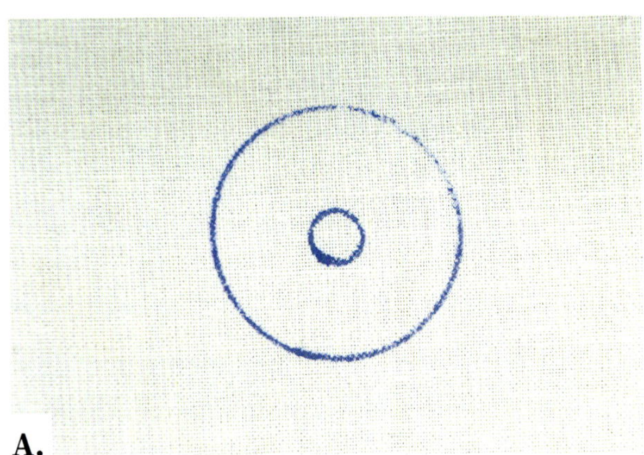

A.

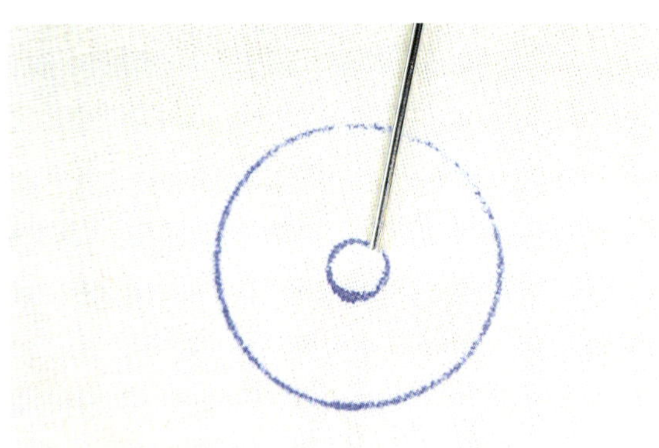

B.

2. Insert the needle into the outer circle (B) along the line of stitching and back up close to where the first stitch was made. (C) *fig. C*

3. Pass the needle through and over the loop. *fig. D*

4. Gently tighten the loop. *fig. E*

5. Continue making blanket stitches in this manner around the circle. *fig. F*

6. At the end of the circle, insert the needle into the fabric where the first stitch came out (A). *fig. G*

7. Tighten the last stitch to finish the circle.

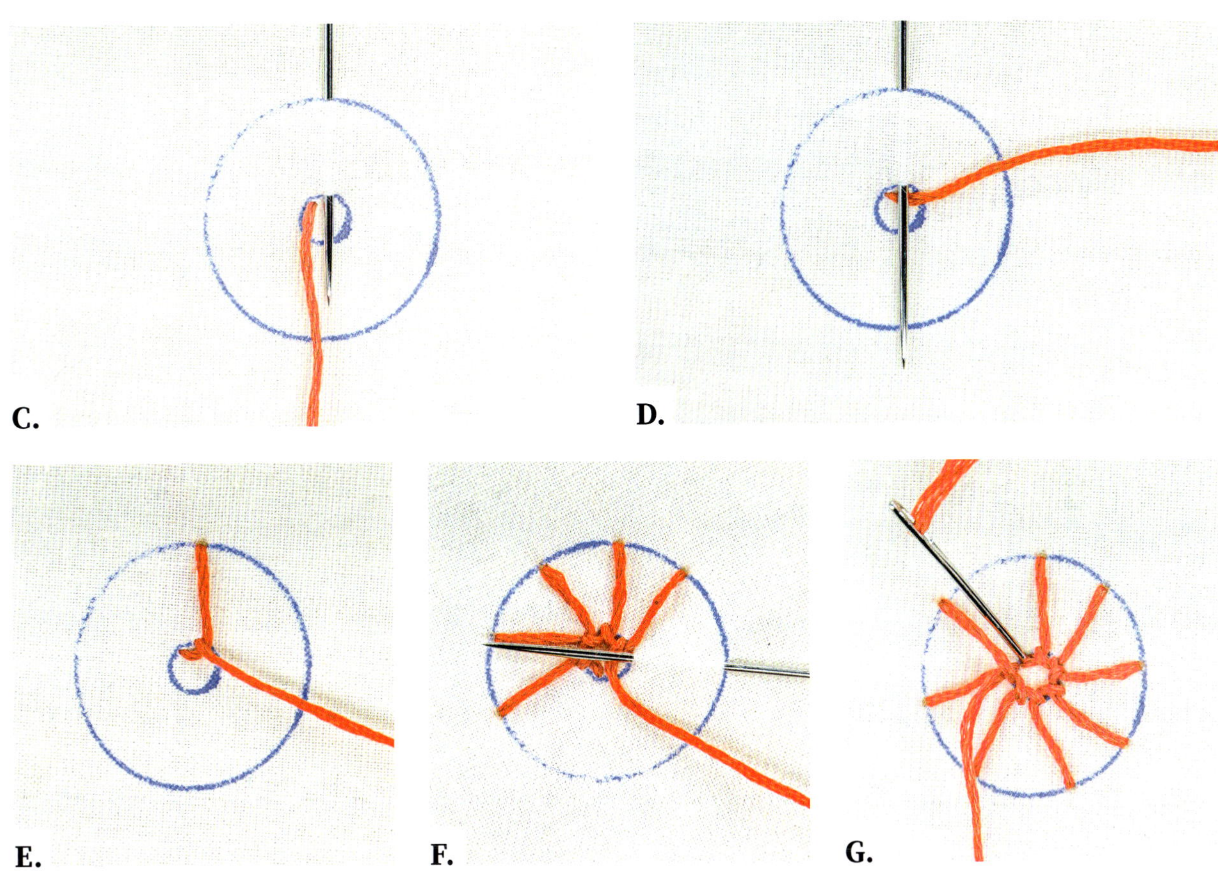

C. D. E. F. G.

BLANKET STITCH WHEEL

Yet another blanket stitch variation that turns the blanket stitch sunburst (page 58) inside out creating a wheel with spokes. Don't ask us to choose a favorite ... that just wouldn't be fair!

For practice, it is helpful to mark a roundish shape with a single point in the center. All stitches will come out of the single center point, creating a hole at this point. If the fabric is weak or thin, this can cause a larger hole, so we reserve this for thicker fabric, stable fabric, layers of fabric, and patches. *fig. A*

1. Start by bringing the needle up on the outside circle (A). *fig. B*

2. Insert the needle into the center mark (B) and back up on the outer circle (C) along the line of stitching while holding the working thread in a loose loop. *fig. C*

3. Pass the needle through and over the loop. *fig. D*

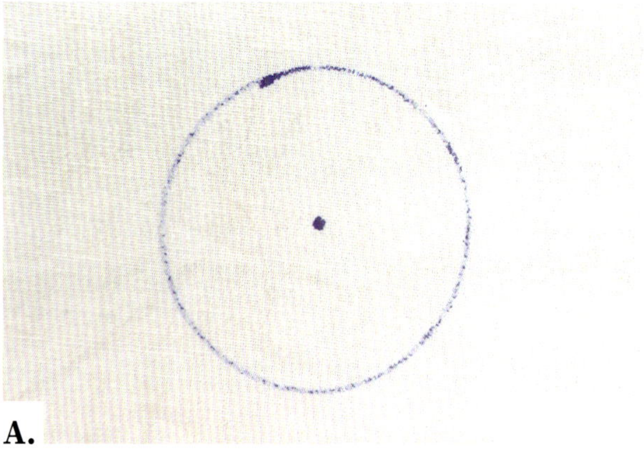

A.

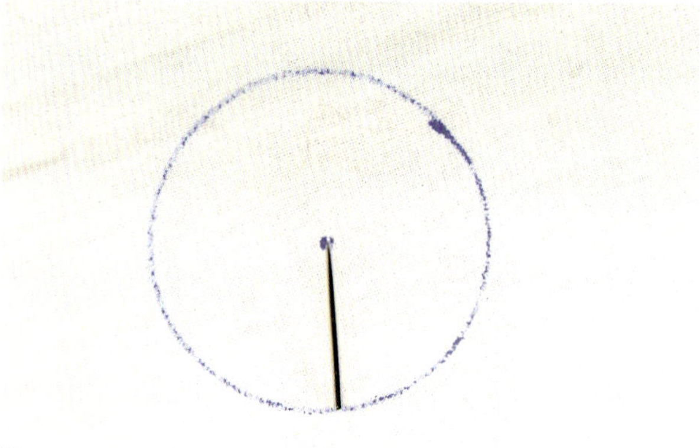

B.

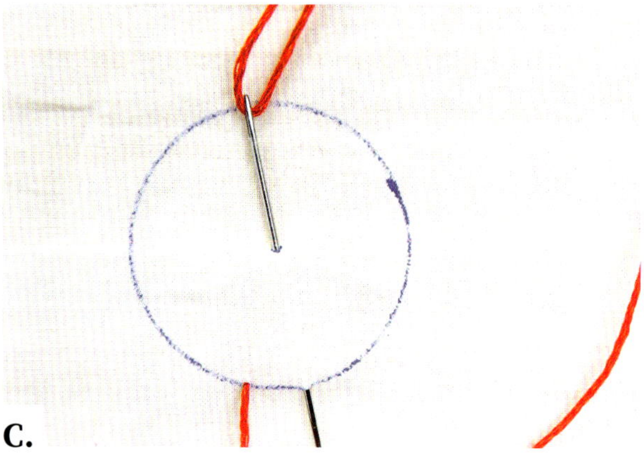

C.

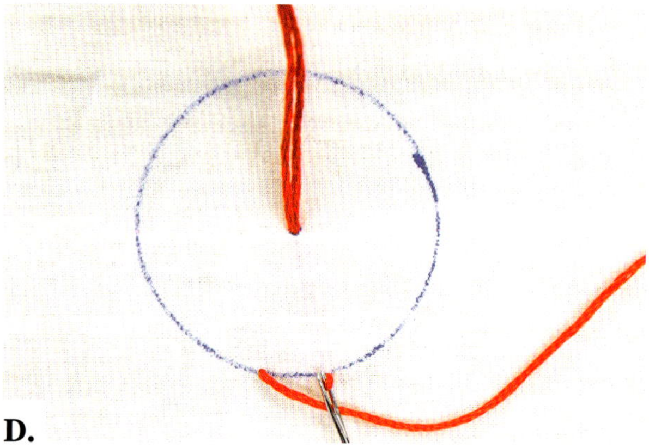

D.

4. Gently tighten the loop, being careful not to pucker the fabric. First wheel spoke made. *fig. E*

5. Insert the needle into the center of the wheel where the first stitch was made (B) and back up on the outer circle (D) along the direction of stitching.

6. Pass the needle through and over the loop, tightening as before. Second wheel spoke made. *fig. F*

7. Continue in this manner until the last stitch of the circle. *fig. G*

8. At the end of the circle, bring the needle up on the outer circle where the first outer stitch was made. (A) *fig. H*

9. Pass the needle through and over the loop and gently tighten as before. *fig. I*

10. Make a single small stitch over the loop to secure.

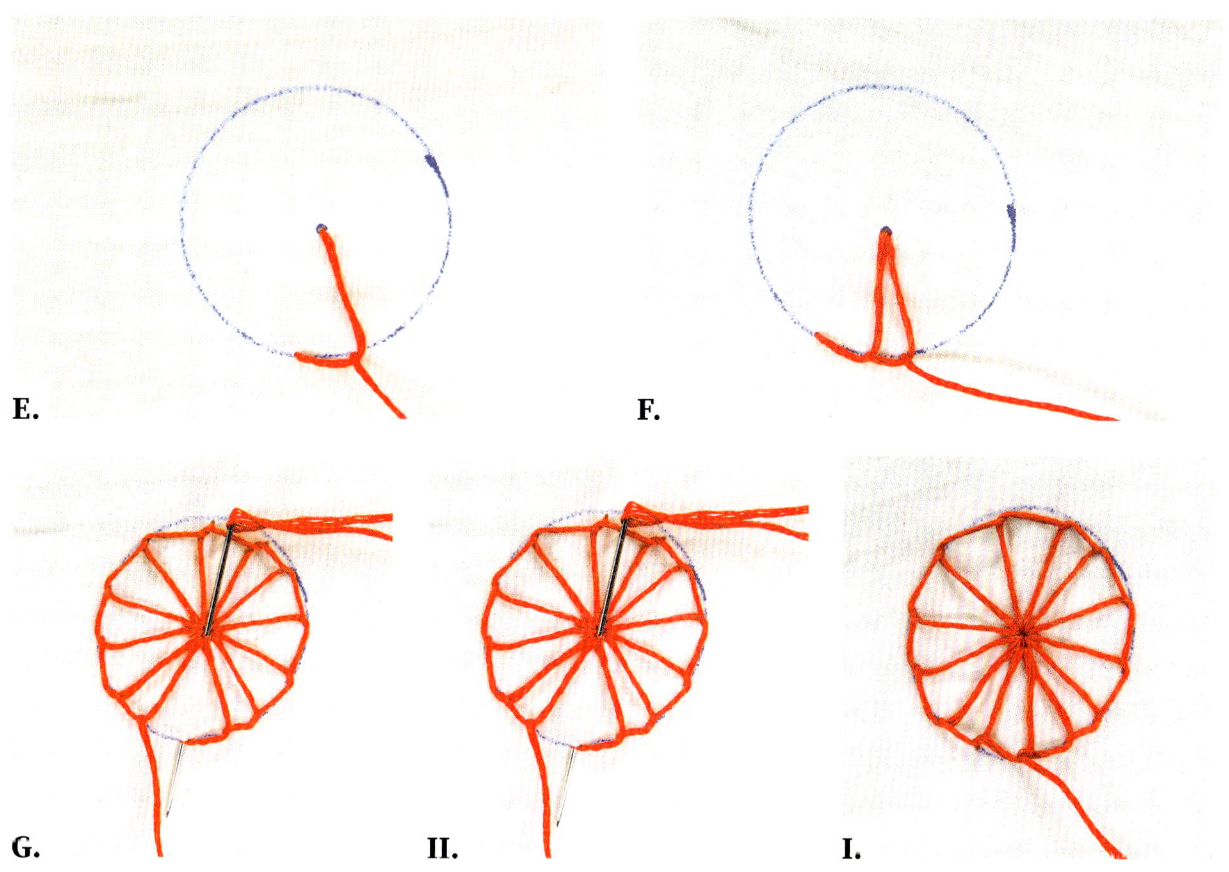

E. **F.** **G.** **H.** **I.**

TAILOR'S BUTTONHOLE STITCH

As the name says, this is the stitch to use if you want to finish the edges of a buttonhole or add a pop of color to your buttonholes with a contrasting thread color. Because it is so great at securing an edge, it is also perfect for patches and securing the edges of holes that will be left open and visible in a mend. *fig. A*

1. Make a small tack stitch at the beginning of the line of stitching. If there is a fold in the fabric or layers of fabric, such as with a patch and base fabric, bring the needle up from inside the fold or layers. *fig. B*
2. Bring the needle up a short distance inside the edge of the fabric or the patch (A). It is helpful when practicing to use fabric with a visible weave or to draw a line to keep these stitches even. *fig. C*
3. Wrap the working thread toward yourself and around the needle counterclockwise. *fig. D*

A.

B.

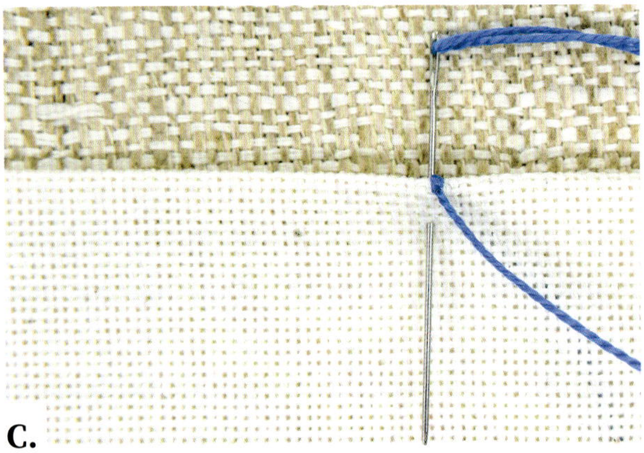

C.

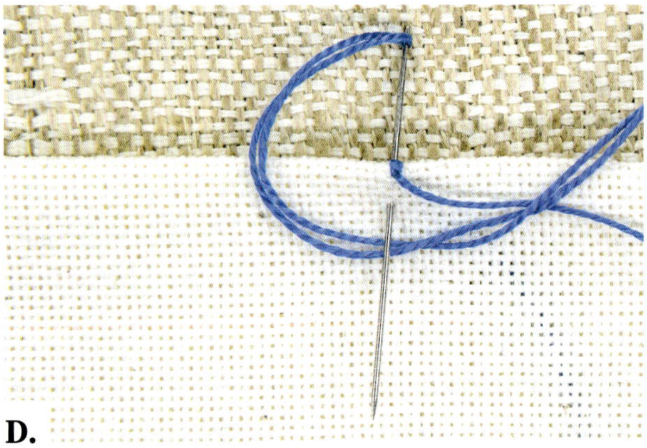

D.

4a. Pull the needle through and tighten the stitch by first pulling the working thread away from the edge of the fabric ... *fig. E*

4b. ... and then toward the edge of the fabric so the resulting knot sits directly on the edge. *fig. F*

5. Move the needle along the edge of the fabric and bring it up right next to the previous stitch (D). This ensures that the stitches create a solid line of stitching that secures the edge of the fabric. *fig. G*

6. Repeat steps 3, 4a, and 4b. Notice how the knots are lying right next to each other, creating a secure edge. *fig. H*

7. Continue in this manner to the end of the line of stitching.

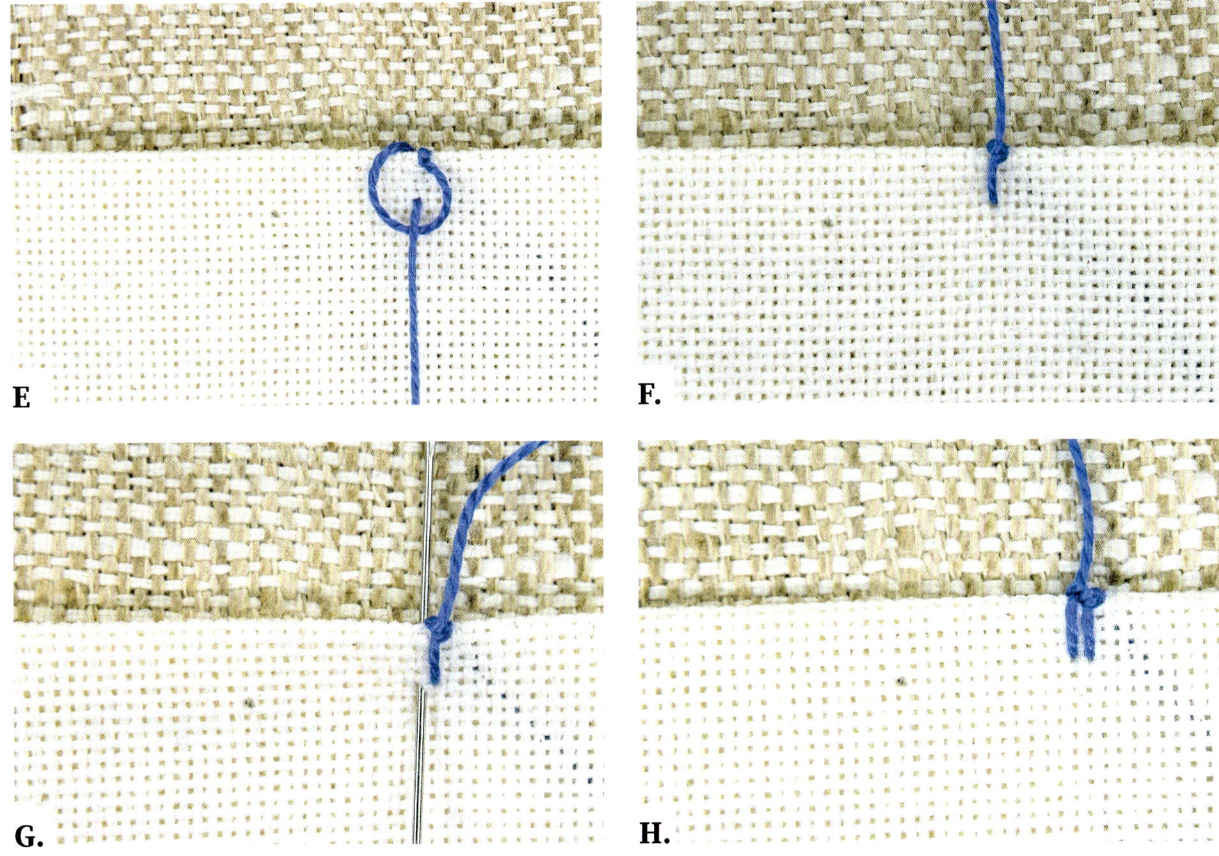

OVERLOCK STITCH

The overlock stitch is another functionally strong but esthetically pleasing stitch for securing the edges of fabric and appliqué patches. The trick is to work between half the strands of the working threads. For example, if working with two threads held together, the needle will pass between those two threads. If working with four threads held together, the needle will pass between two sets of two threads, six strands will be three and three, and so forth.

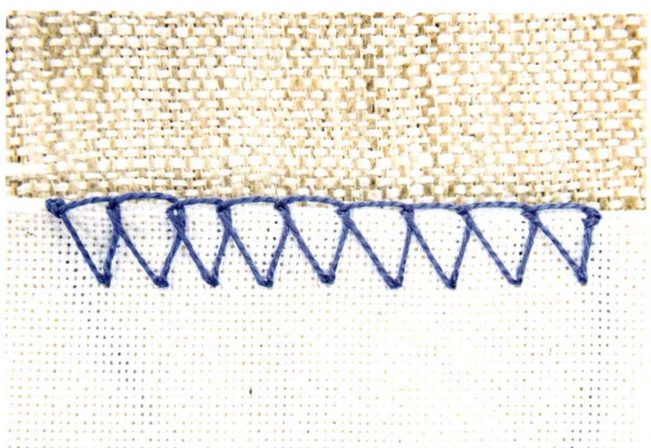

1. Make a starting tack stitch at the beginning of the line of stitching (A) and insert the needle back into the fabric a short distance away (B). Leave a loop on top of the fabric. *fig. A*

2. Insert the needle into the fabric diagonally from the stitch just made along the line of stitching. (D) *fig. B*

3. Bring the needle up at the edge of the patch or fabric (E) and pass it between the strands of thread. *fig. C*

4. Pull this stitch snug, creating a small triangle with the strand of thread caught by the working thread and the loose loop. *fig. D*

5. Repeat Steps 2–4 to the end of the line of stitching, ensuring that as you pass between the threads they are not twisted. Secure the final stitch with a tack stitch.

Note • Livin' on the Edge

Be sure to maintain even tension when using stitches like the overlock stitch to secure the edge of a piece of fabric. Pulling these stitches too tightly over the edge of the fabric will result in puckering that just won't look cute. At all.

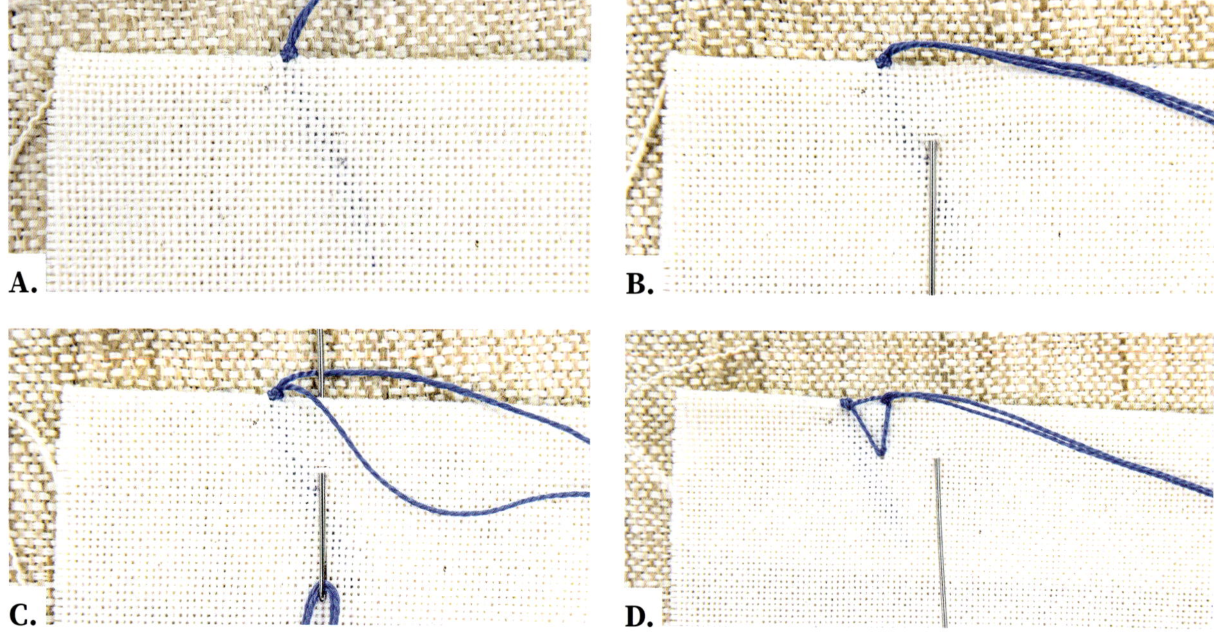

A. B. C. D.

SATIN STITCH

The satin stitch, while highly decorative and used for filling designs, is also a dense stitch perfect for covering all manner of small holes, stains, scorches, and splatters. Use it as a jumping-off point to create a mend that is not just visible but *FAB*. The satin stitch is best worked on hooped fabric with a dense weave and with a drawn outline to follow.

Fill in the shape by laying parallel stitches as close together as possible without crossing or overlapping. *fig. A*

For shapes like squares and rectangles, start at one side and work across until the shape is filled. *fig. B*

For irregular shapes, it is best to start at the center and work out in either direction.

The first few stitches can be made first on one side of the central line and then on the other side, alternating for the first three to five stitches. *fig. C*

Next, fill in one side of the shape. *fig. D*

Finally, fill in the opposite side.

For shapes worked to one direction and then the next, either tie off the thread and start again on the opposite side or, for smaller shapes, run the needle beneath the stitches on the back of the mend. In the case of the satin stitch shown here, the working thread is woven around the edge stitches of the circle. *fig. E*

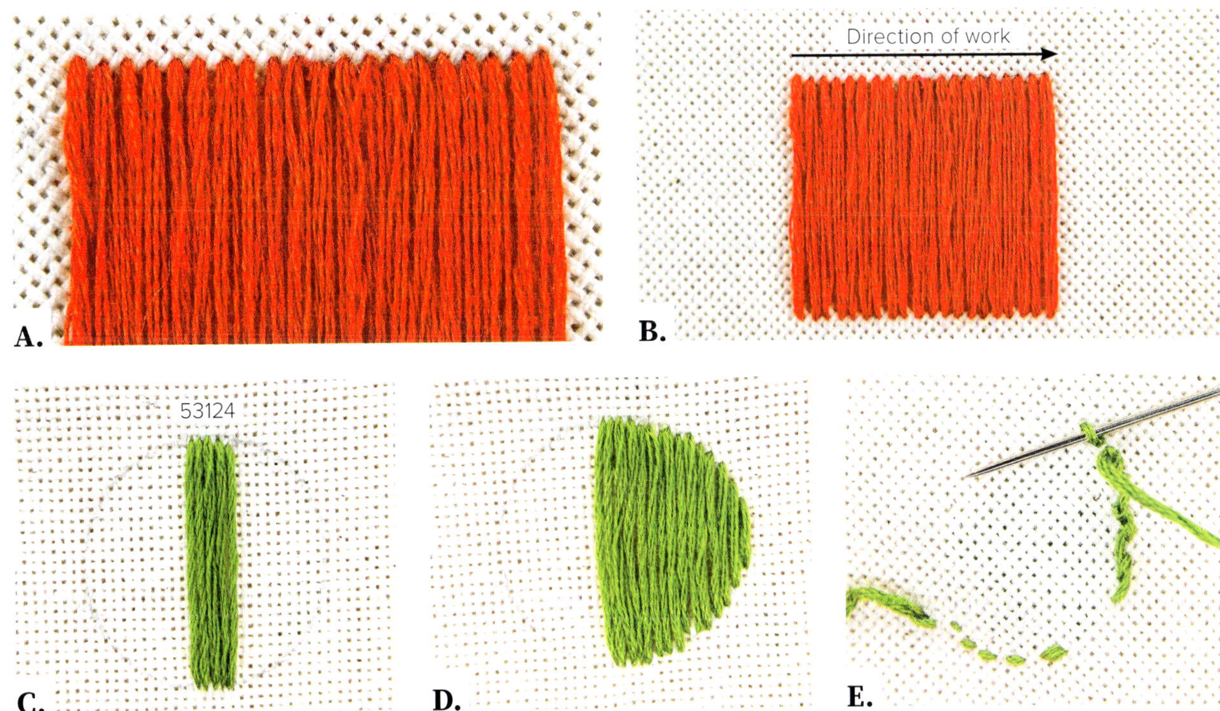

A. B. C. D. E.

BRICK STITCH

The brick stitch is a great fabric stabilizer and, when combined with a patch, makes a fabric that is stronger than the original. This stitch is dense and has a beautiful texture to it.

1. Start by making a row of backstitch. See Backstitch (page 30). *fig. A*
2. Now make a row of backstitch where the stitches are offset from the previous row. Note that the first and last stitch of this row are shorter. (B) *fig. B*
3. Continue making rows of offset backstitches until the mend area is filled. (C)

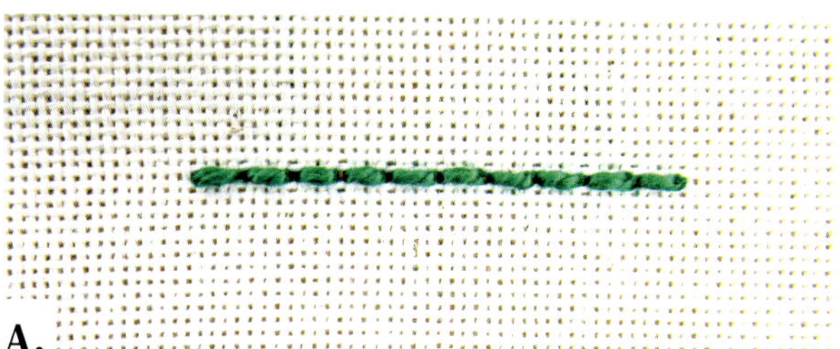

A.

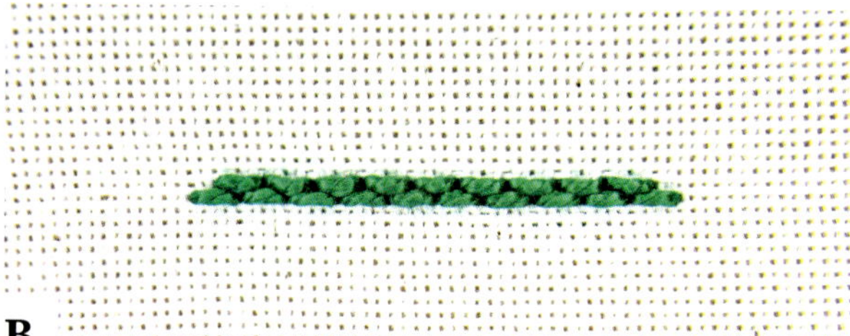

B.

FEATHER STITCH

The feather stitch is a common stitch for crazy quilting and for botanical embroidery. We love it for covering a mend to help disguise the fact that it is ... well ... a mend!

1. Bring the needle up at (A) and down at (B), leaving a loose loop. *fig. A*
2. Bring the needle back up at (C), catching the loop with the working thread. *fig. B*

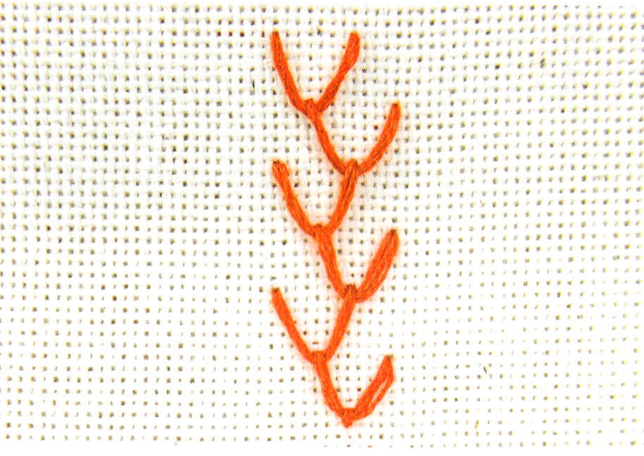

A.

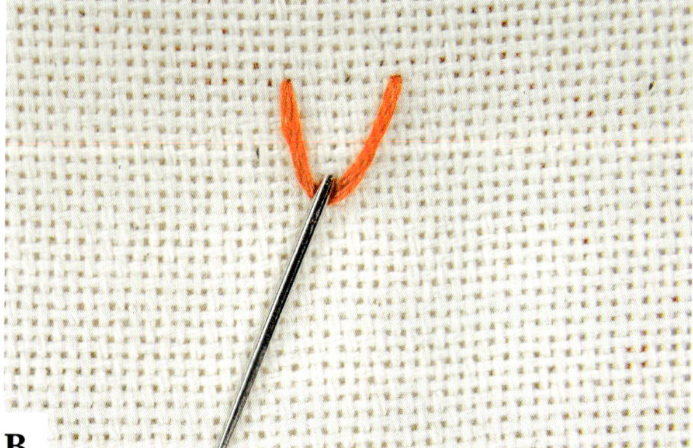

B.

3. Insert the needle into the fabric at (D), again leaving a loop. *fig. C*
4. Bring the needle back up at (E), catching the loop with the working thread. *fig. D*
5. Repeat until the desired length of pattern is reached. To end, make a tack stitch in the center of the last loop.

The feather stitch works beautifully as an organic curved botanical feature, giving it the look of seaweed or grasses. *fig. E*

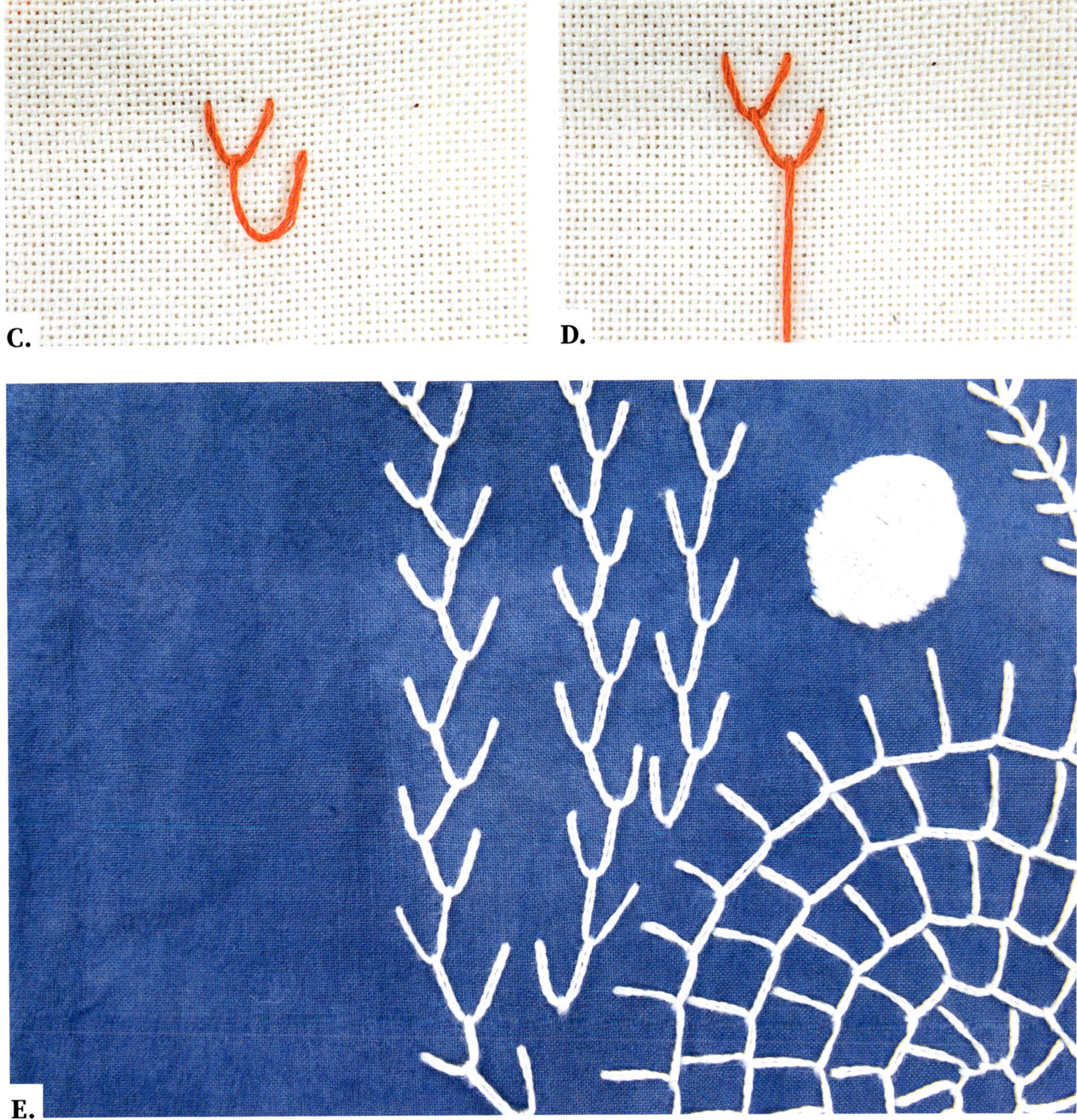

C. **D.** **E.**

DETACHED CHAIN STITCH

These stitches work beautifully for filling an area with a random scatter effect. Use these to hold a patch in place for a secure mend.

1. Make a single chain stitch and finish with a small tack stitch as if you were ending a row of chain stitches (see Chain Stitch, page 44). *fig. A*

2. Continue to make detached chain stitches at random angles and places until the area is filled.

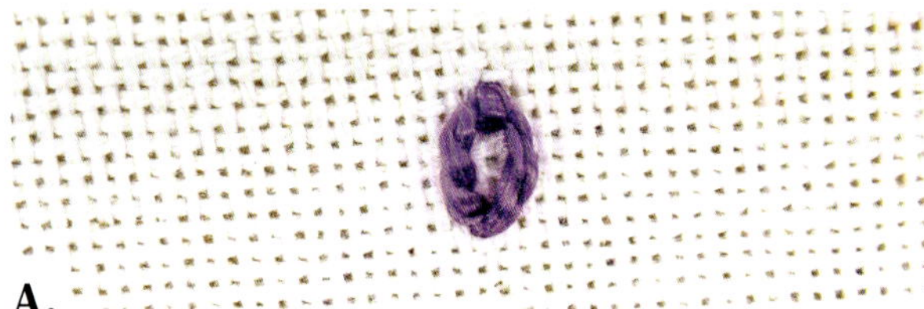
A.

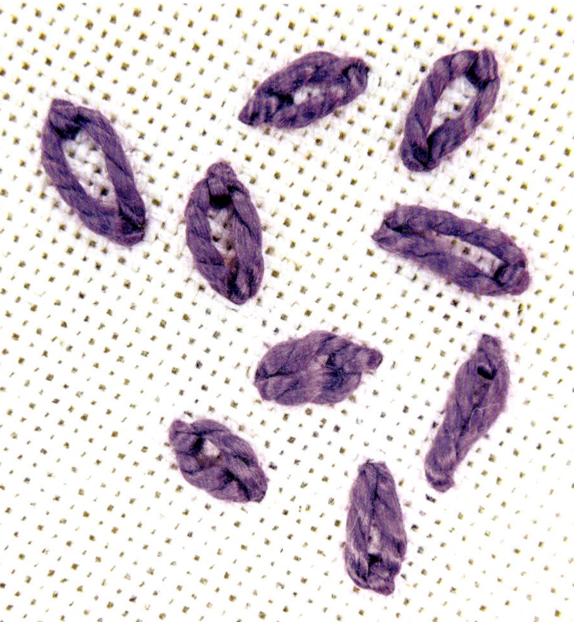

LAZY DAISY STITCH

While the detached chain stitch is great for randomized, scattered filling of patterns, the lazy daisy uses the detached chain stitch in a more floral arrangement.

1. Mark the area with a central point and spokes as shown. *fig. A*

2. Make a detached chain stitch by bringing the needle up at the central point and placing the tack stitch at the end of the first spoke. *fig. B*

3. Make the next petal of the flower by bringing the needle up again at the central point and place the tack stitch at the end of the next spoke. *fig. C*

4. Continue to fill in the spokes of the flower.

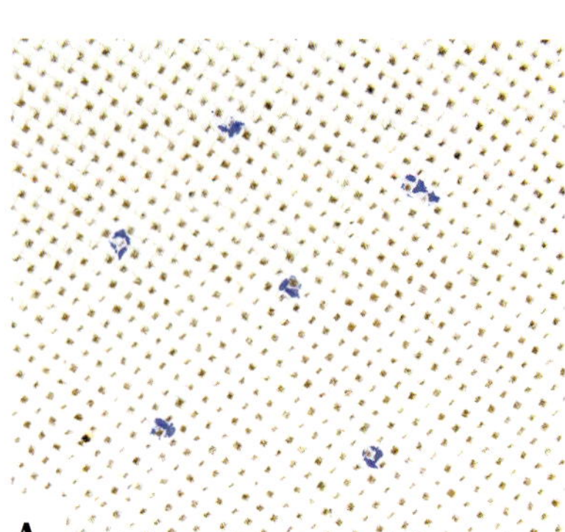
A.

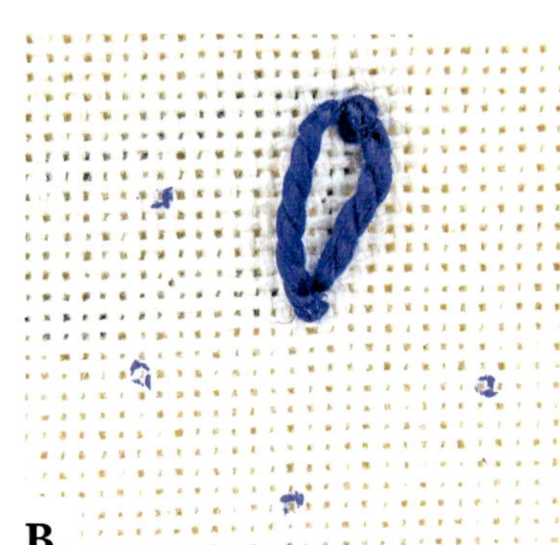
B.

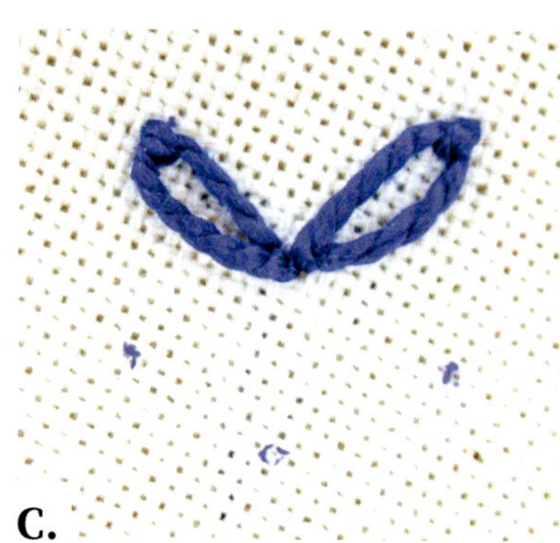
C.

FERN STITCH

The fern stitch is another stitch that can be used as a filler and decorator stitch or as a way to define the outline of a shape. The line of central stitches also makes the fern stitch an unexpected border that will secure a patch with style.

1. Start by bringing the needle up at (A) and back down at (B) on the central line. If securing a patch, this is the stitch line that will secure the edge of the patch. *fig. A*
2. Bring the needle back up at (C) and back down at (B) again. *fig. B*
3. Bring the needle up at (D) and back down at (B) again. *fig. C*
4. Bring the needle up at (E) and back down again at (B). *fig. D*

A.

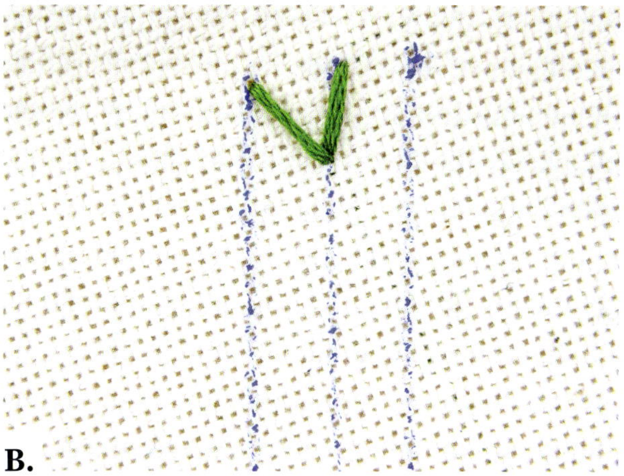

B.

C.

D.

5. Bring the needle up at (F) and back down at (E). *fig. E*

6. Bring the needle up at (G) and back down again at (E). *fig. F*

7. Repeat Steps 4–6 until the end of the line is reached. *fig. G*

The fern stitch works beautifully as an organic curved pattern. *fig. H*

E. **F.** **G.** **H.**

FRENCH KNOT

French knots are a staple of embroidery as fine filling stitches. Worked in multiple colors, the stitches can look like confetti or be used to shade the colors of a design or shape. And, of course, as the name indicates, they are fancy knots made on the surface of the fabric, meaning each stitch will secure a patch very effectively. The saying is definitely true with French knots: If at first you don't succeed, keep going because this takes practice. Okay ... that's not exactly the saying, but it is true.

1. Bring the needle up from the back of the fabric. *fig. A*
2. Hold the needle close to the fabric and wrap the thread around the needle 3 or 4 times in the direction of the tip of the needle. Be sure to wrap securely but not too tightly. *fig. B*
3. While holding the working thread to the side, insert the needle within a couple of threads of the first stitch. *fig. C*
4. Pull the needle to the back of the fabric and gently pull the thread through the wraps, keeping the tension steady on the working yarn to ensure that the wraps do not unravel. Be sure to hold the working yarn in a loop at tension until it secures the wraps, making the final knot. *fig. D*

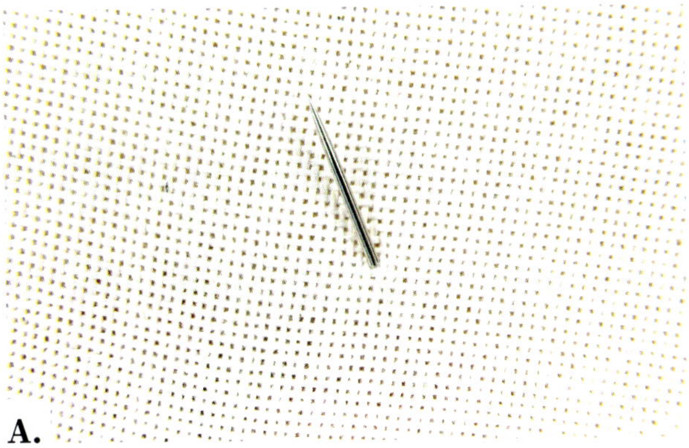

A.

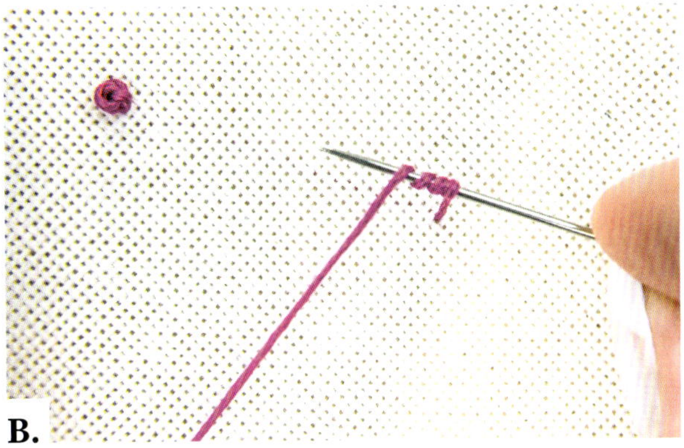

B.

C.

D.

5. Pull the thread snug to secure the knot. *fig. E*

6. Continue making knots on the surface of the fabric to fill the mend or until the desired effect is achieved.

E.

Note • Does It Really Matter?

If the French knot knots are not large enough, use additional strands of thread or a heavier weight thread. But bigger isn't always better! Alternating weights of thread in a single section gives the overall pattern texture and visual interest.

SEED STITCH (RICE STITCH)

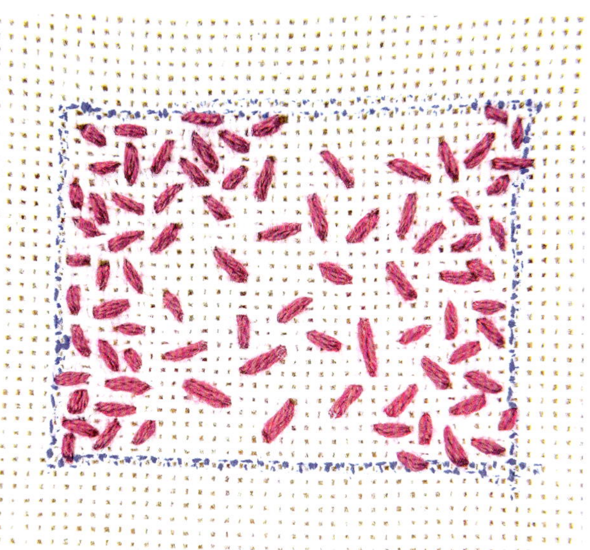

The seed stitch is an efficient filling stitch. Once a rhythm is achieved, the stitches fill a space quickly and will securely hold a patch.

Begin by marking the area to be filled.

1. Bring the needle up anywhere inside of the defined mending area (A) and back down a short distance away. (B) *fig. A*

2. Make another stitch of the same(ish) length near the first stitch but at a different angle. *fig. B*

3. Continue to make short stitches, randomizing the angle at which they are placed to resemble scattered seeds or scattered grains of rice.

Vary the distance of the stitches to create a difference in density.

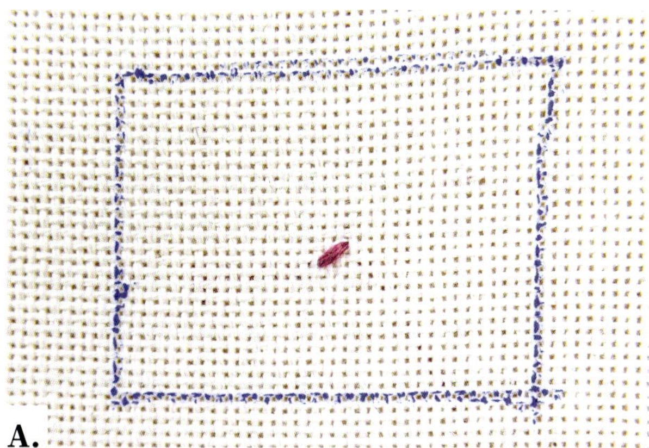

A.

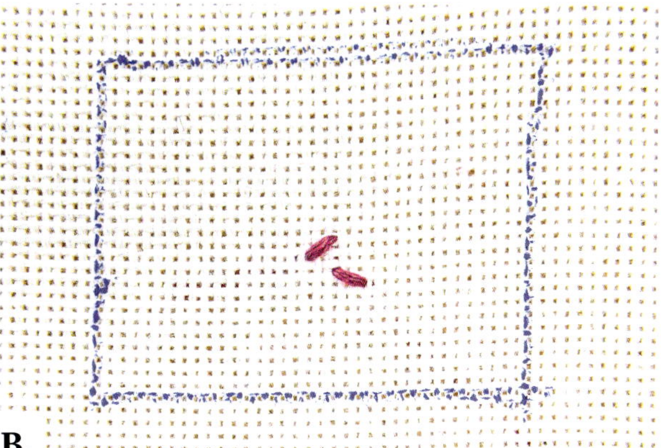

B.

STAR STITCH

The star stitch is such a simple little stitch but makes a big impact for decorating a mend and holding a patch in place.

Define the area to be stitched by drawing a small circle.

1. Bring the needle up at one edge of the circle (A) and back down directly across the circle. (B) *fig. A*
2. Now make a stitch the same way, crossing the first stitch. *fig. B*
3. Make another stitch that reaches diagonally across the first cross made. *fig. C*
4. Finish this second cross. *fig. D*
5. Continue to make stars of different sizes until the area is filled. Alter the look of the stars by making some crosses shorter and some longer.

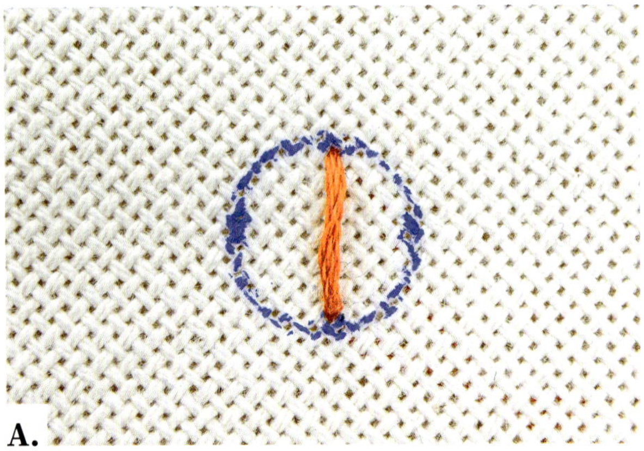

A.

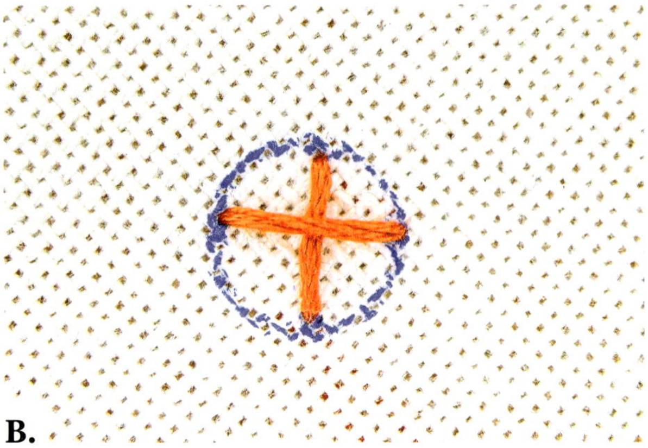

B.

C.

D.

WEAVE STITCH

The weave stitch is great for knits but not JUST knits. While we use this stitch for beautiful and functional mends on knit fabrics, the density and the ability to vary the look with different types of thread or yarn makes it a beautiful mending stitch for all types of fabrics. This versatile stitch also works as a filler stitch for shapes and designs.

Weave stitch in two colors with the vertical stitches in one color and the horizontal woven stitches in a second color

1. Start by making vertical, closely placed, parallel stitches. Bring the needle up at (A) then down at (B); bring the needle up again at (C) close to (B) and down at (D). *fig. A*

2. Continue to fill the mending area with vertical stitches. *fig. B*

3. Now begin weaving the horizontal stitches. Bring the needle up at (E) and use the eye of the needle to weave the needle over and under each thread to the end of the row. Insert the needle back into the fabric (F) at the end of the weaving row. To make this easier, we use a long darning needle or a bent-tip embroidery needle. *fig. C*

4. For the next row, bring the needle up (G) and weave the needle over and under each thread alternating the previous rows' stitches. If a stitch passed under on the previous row, this row will pass over. If a stitch passed over on the previous row, the stitch will pass under on this row. Continue to weave to the end of the row. Insert the needle back into the fabric (H) at the end of the weaving row.

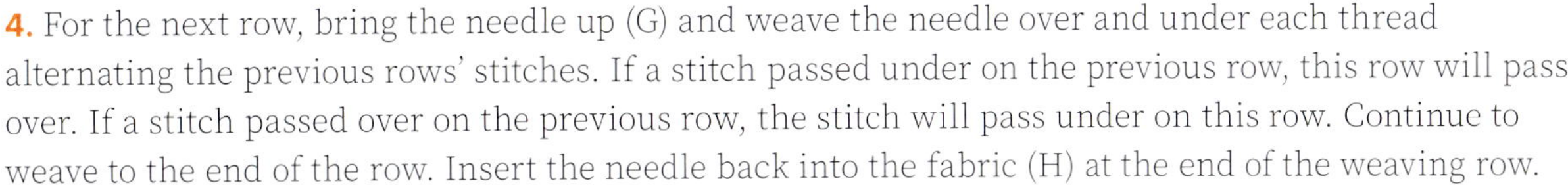

The perpendicular rows should be spaced roughly 2 times the distance of the vertical rows. This will vary depending on your chosen thread. *fig. D*

5. Continue weaving horizontal rows until the area is filled.

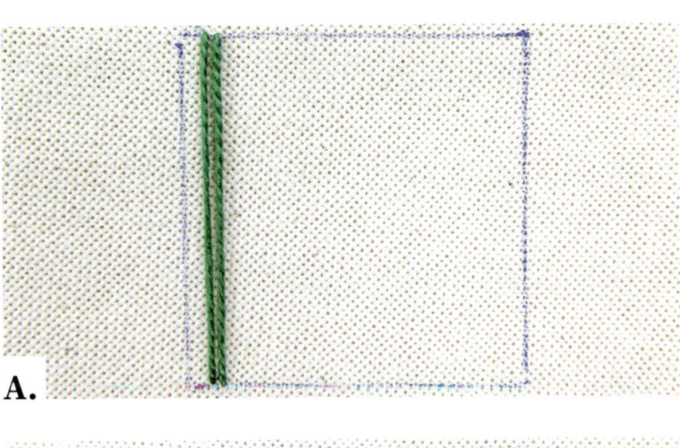

A.

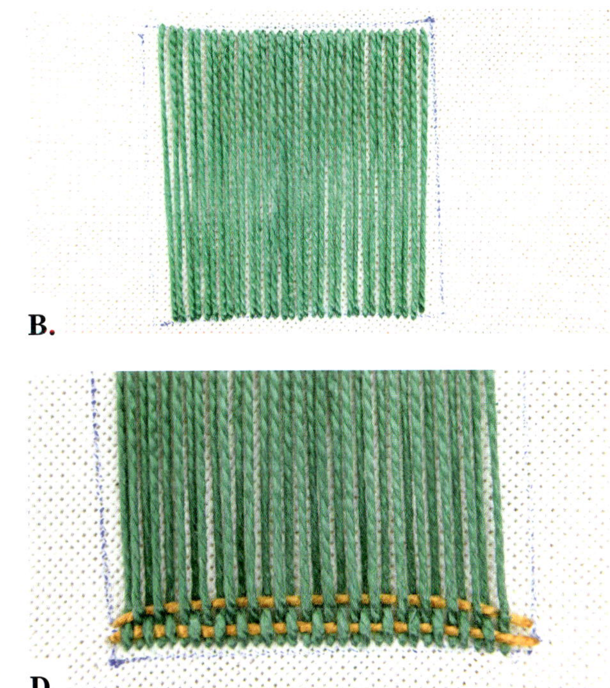

B.

C.

D.

SPIDER WHEEL (WHIPPED WHEEL)

Decorative? Yes. Functional? Also yes. Like so many other stitches that have a central anchor point, the spokes of the spider wheel secure patches with multiple close stitches. The decorative pattern emerges when a whipstitch is used to encase each spoke. Any number of spokes can make up the spider wheel as long as they are evenly spaced. The whipstitches are best worked using a blunt-tipped needle or pass the needle under the spokes with the eye of the needle.

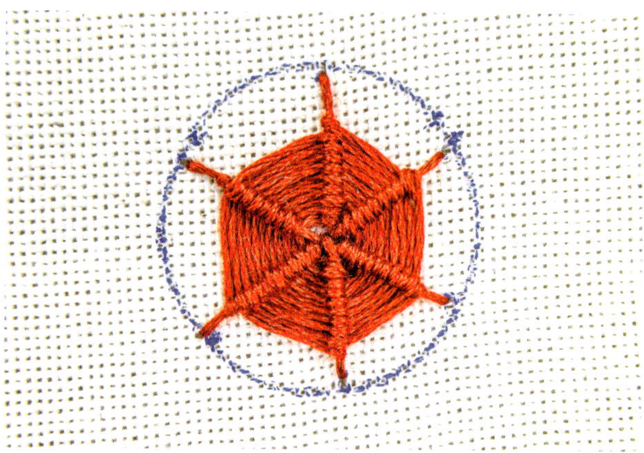

1. Begin by marking a circle the desired size of the wheel. *fig. A*
2. Bring the needle up at the center of the circle and down at the outside of the circle. *fig. B*
3. Bring the needle up again at the center and down at the outside of the circle directly across from the stitch just made. *fig. C*
4. Repeat until you have an even number of spokes. Our example uses 6 spokes. *fig. D*

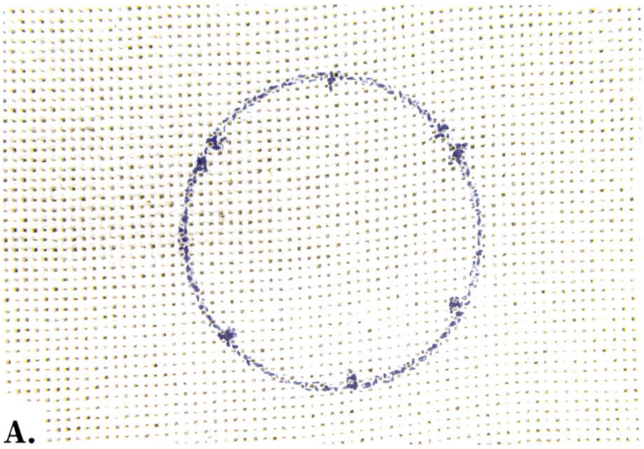

A.

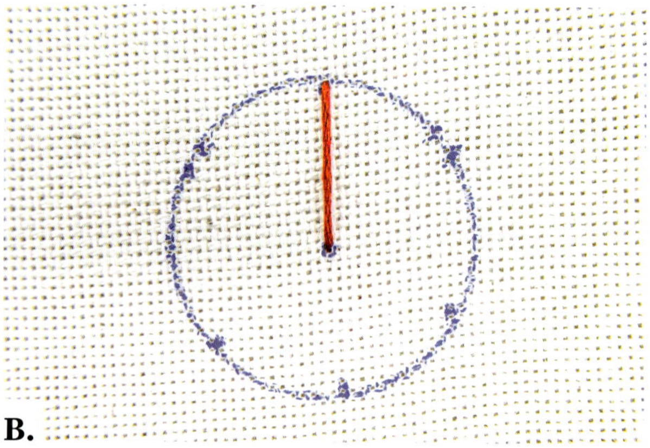

B.

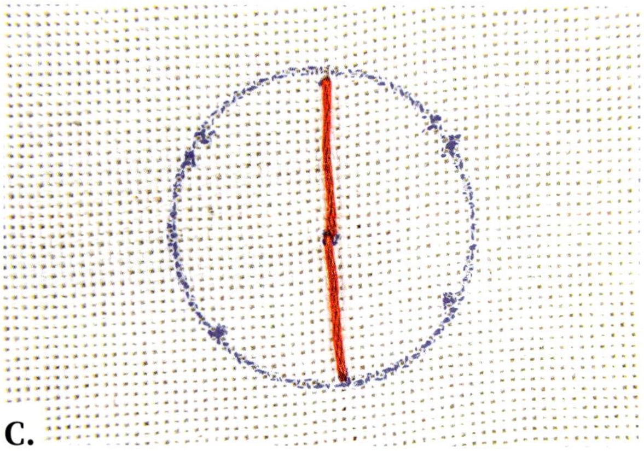

C.

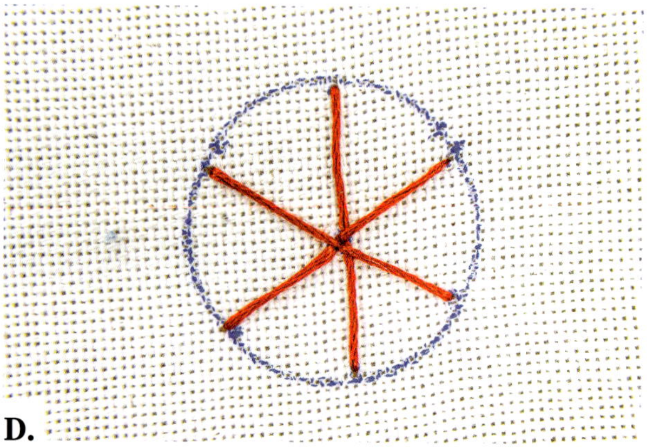

D.

5. Bring the needle up through the center once more. *fig. E*

6. Now switch to a blunt-tipped needle or use the eye of the needle to whipstitch around the spokes of the wheel. Pass the needle under the first spoke. *fig. F*

7. Wrap back under the first spoke and the neighboring second spoke, creating a whipstitch around the first spoke. Make sure this wrap is snug to the center of the wheel. *fig. G*

8. Pass the needle over the second spoke and under the second and third spokes, wrapping the thread around the second spoke. Again, snug the wrapped stitch to the center of the wheel. Use the needle to snug the wrap if needed. *fig. H*

9. Continue to work whipstitches around each spoke until all spokes are wrapped. Then stack the wraps and strands outward until the spokes are filled.

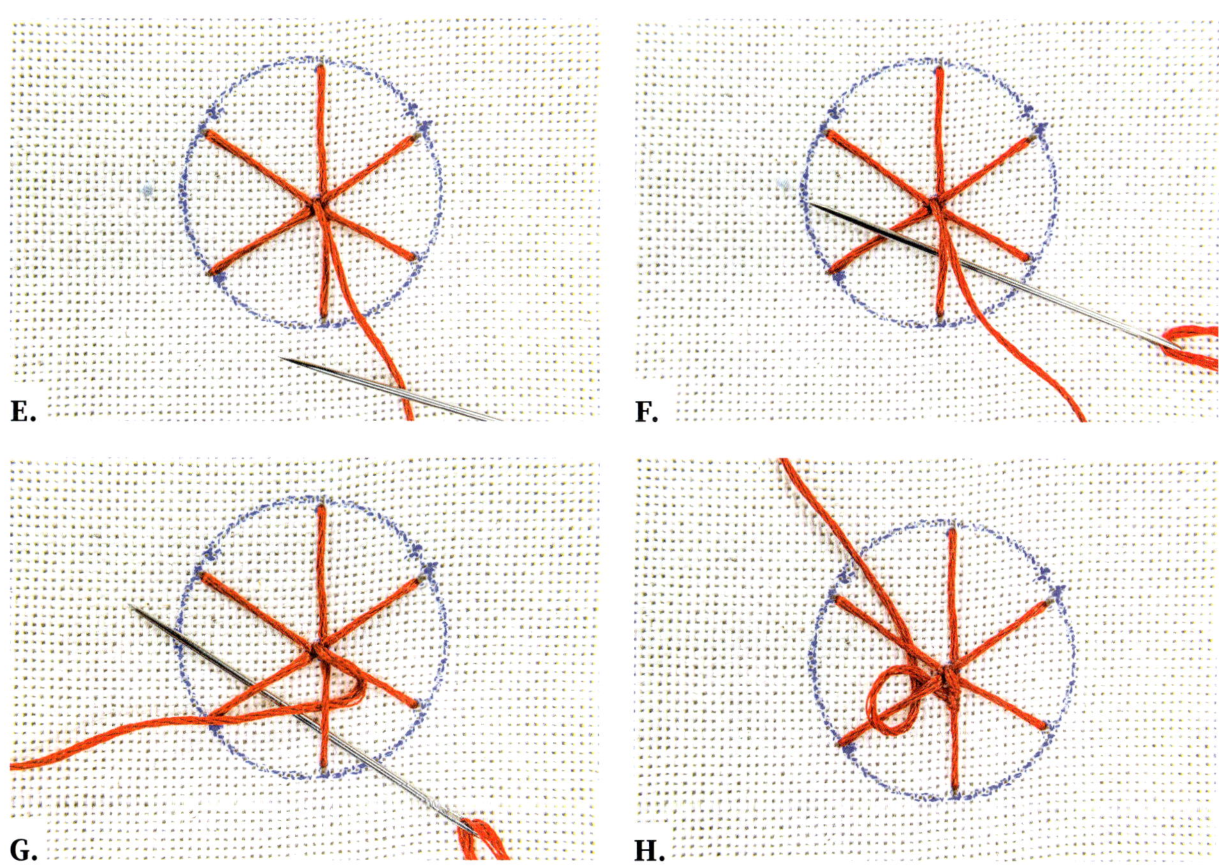

ROSE WHEEL (WOVEN WHEEL)

The rose wheel is a cousin to the spider wheel with a dramatically different result. The starting point of creating a spoked wheel achieves the same result of a stitch that secures patched areas but looks beautiful. Since this stitch is created by weaving, there must be an odd number of spokes for the woven technique to work properly. Try this one with variegated thread or a fluffy yarn to enhance the look of a rose.

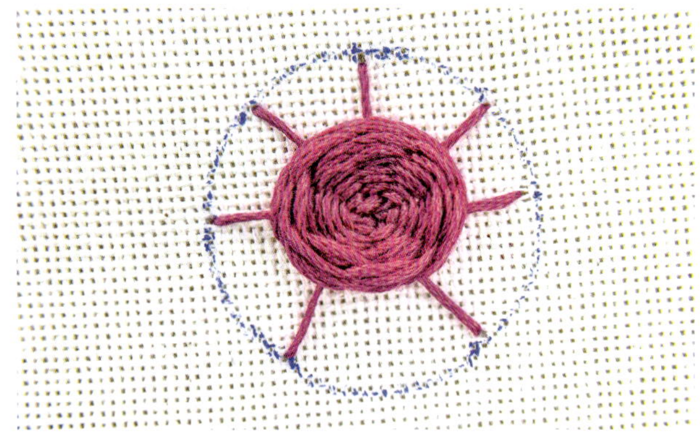

1. Begin by making a wheel with an odd number of spokes using Steps 1–5 of the spider wheel stitch (page 76). *fig. A*
2. With a blunt-tipped needle, pass the thread over the first spoke and under the second. *fig. B*
3. Pull the thread snug close to the center of the spokes. *fig. C*
4. Pass the needle over the third spoke and under the fourth and snug the thread. *fig. D*
5. Continue weaving around the spokes of the wheel until the spokes are filled.

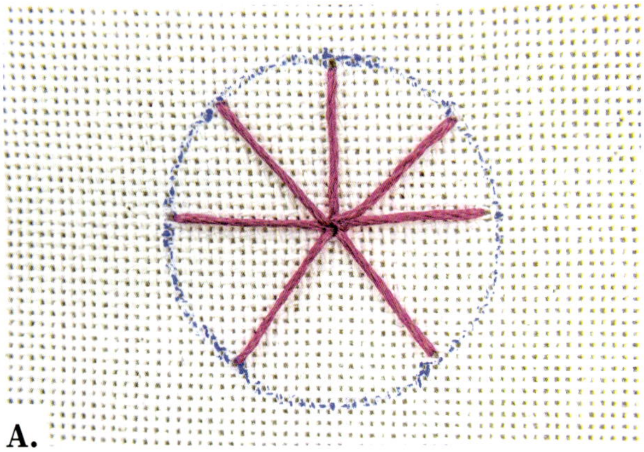

A.

B.

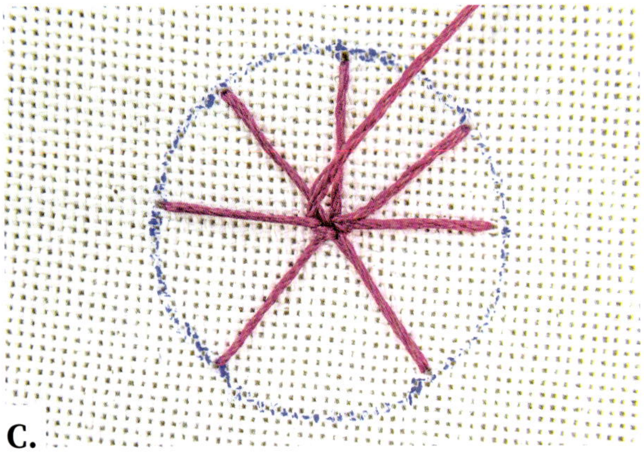

C.

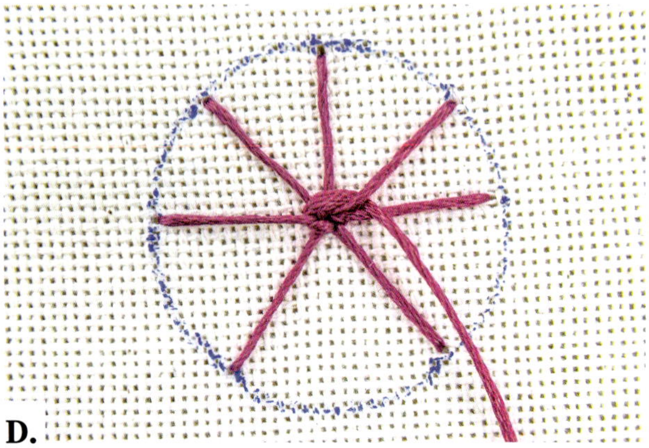

D.

BACKSTITCH TRELLIS

The backstitch trellis uses a network of backstitches to create a secure mend. Use this over a patch or to reinforce a weak fabric. To assist with creating a neat trellis, draw a square grid over the mend area.

1. Begin by outlining the area to be filled and draw a grid or use evenweave embroidery fabric to stitch your trellis.

2. Use the backstitch to create a diagonal line across the widest part of the mend (see Backstitch, page 30). *fig. A*

3. Continue to make backstitch diagonal lines parallel to the first line, filling in first one side of the mend area and then the other. *figs. B-C*

4. Now make a backstitch diagonal line running perpendicular to the first set of lines. This first line will be across the widest part of the mend. Note that the needle will be coming up and down through the holes previously made by the first set of stitches. *fig. D*

5. As before, continue to make backstitch rows filling the rest of the mend area.

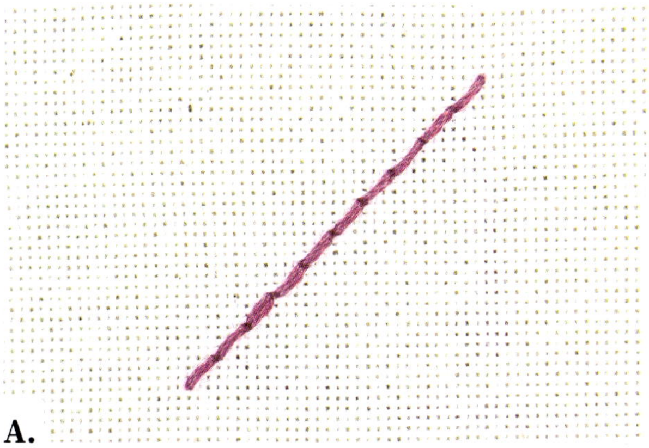

A.

B.

C.

D.

SASHIKO

Sashiko began as a traditional Japanese stitching method for mending and reinforcement. What started as a functional practice, through the lens of time, became an art form. Sashiko stitches are perfect for securing patches, as well as for reinforcing fabric that is worn by essentially filling the fabric with stitches that act to reweave the fabric. Often sashiko stitchers will use a simple chart for following a pattern.

Sashiko charts will generally include:

- A background grid to get you started
- Lines to indicate where visible stitches originate and terminate
- Numbers to indicate the order the rows of stitches are worked
- Arrows indicating the direction of work in relation to the finished stitch pattern
- Occasionally, dotted lines to indicate moving to the next row where the thread is carried under the fabric, connecting two lines of stitches (not necessarily in rows)

In this book, we included the main sashiko stitches that we use for most common mends. To go deeper down the sashiko rabbit hole, check out our book *Boro & Sashiko: Harmonious Imperfection,* from C&T Publishing.

HITOMEZASHI

Hitomezashi-style sashiko is based on a small grid with patterns developing from intersecting and crossing lines of stitches.

Hitomezashi designs are made using 1:1 running stitches on even grids—every stitch on the top of the fabric is followed by a stitch on the back of the fabric of the same size. For the most part, we use a ¼″ (6mm) grid for mending (see Hitomezashi Grid, page 90).

Hitomezashi patterns are stitched in a specific order:

1. All horizontal lines
2. All vertical lines
3. All left-leaning diagonal lines
4. All right-leaning diagonal lines

Offset Running Stitch

This chart shows that the offset running stitch pattern is built on a 1:1 grid—the grid blocks are equal in width and height. The numeral 1 with the arrow pointing to the left indicates that Step 1 is to stitch the horizontal rows with the stitch length being the width of one grid space. When you reach the end of the first row, end with your thread below your work and then move up one grid space and on the returning row stitch in the offset spaces from the previous row.

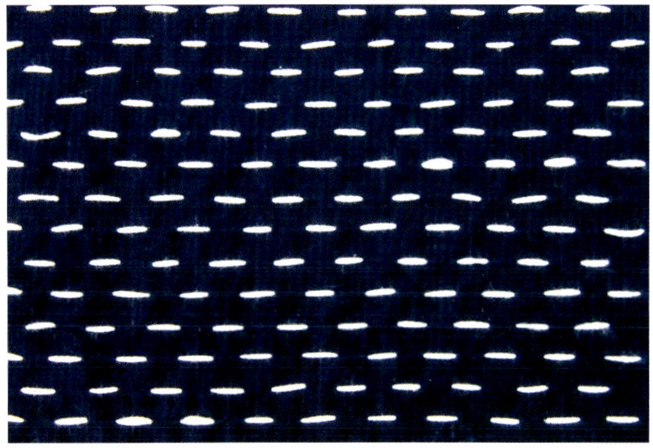

Step 2 shows an arrow pointing up, indicating these are your vertical rows. More to the point, the chart shows you to stitch offset rows directly over the stitches from Step 1. Each stitch originates and terminates in the center of a grid space, the same length as the stitches in Step 1. When you reach the end of the first row, end with your thread below your work and move up one grid space. On your returning row, stitch in the offset spaces from the previous row. Simple enough!

Offset Crosses

This stitch uses offset running stitches as a base to build upon. Going back to the rules we talked about earlier, we know that we do all the horizontal lines, then the vertical lines, then we take on the diagonals, which you can see in the chart by taking note of the numerals 3 and 4 with arrows indicating the direction of the work.

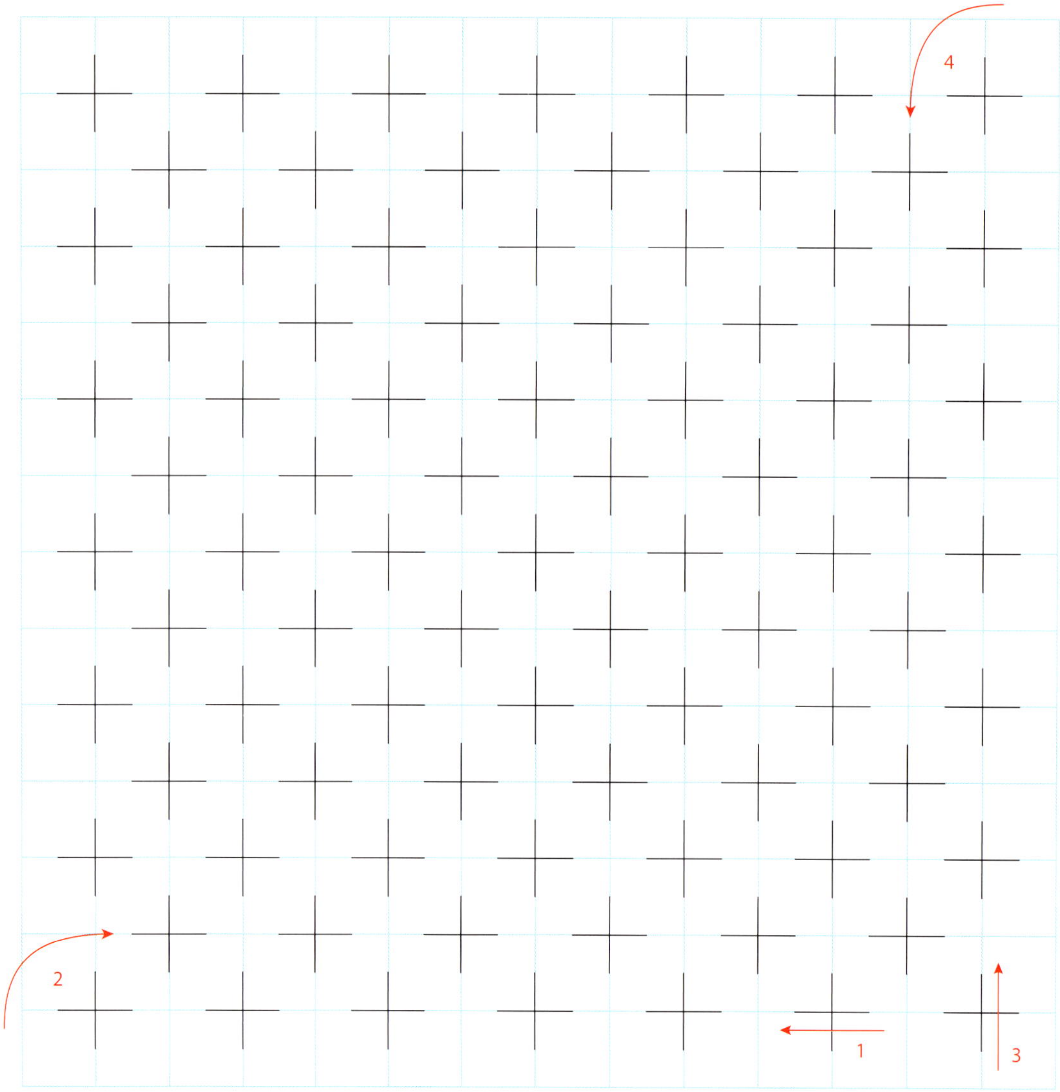

Rice Stitch

Rice stitch adds diagonal lines to the previous offset crosses pattern (at left). Notice that the diagonal lines leave a small space just shy of the center of each cross. They do not start or stop directly under the center point. As a result, your *under-stitch* (the stitch on the back of the fabric) is much smaller than the *over-stitch* (the visible stitch). The only lines that cross are the vertical and horizontal.

MOYOUZASHI

Moyouzashi-style sashiko patterns are based on simple straight or curved lines using as many stitches as needed to get from one point to another. The designs are drawn onto much larger grids compared to hitomezashi (page 90), ratios of inches or centimeters. The size of the ratio can be adjusted to fit your needed area so long as the ratio itself remains intact—for example, a 1:1 ratio can be 1″:1″ (2.5cm:2.5cm) or 1½″:1½″ (3.8cm:3.8cm), and so on. Stitches are usually counted, made as a certain number of stitches from point A to point B on the grid. Lines of moyouzashi stitches never cross on the front of the fabric.

More information about Hitomezashi and Moyouzashi sashiko can be found in our book, *Boro and Sashiko: Harmonious Imperfection,* by C&T Publishing.

Diamonds

Diamonds pattern is drawn on a 1:2 grid—for example, 1″ tall by 2″ wide (2.5 × 5.1cm).

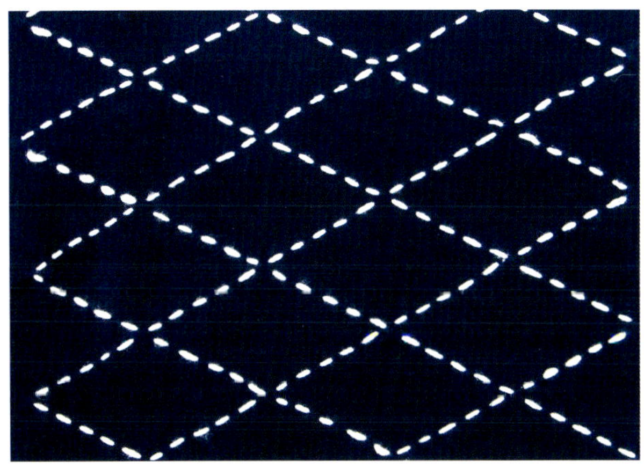

1

2

Blue Ocean Waves

Blue ocean waves is drawn on a 1:1 grid—for example, 1″ tall by 1″ wide (2.5 × 2.5cm). We recommend using a circle template to draw the circles.

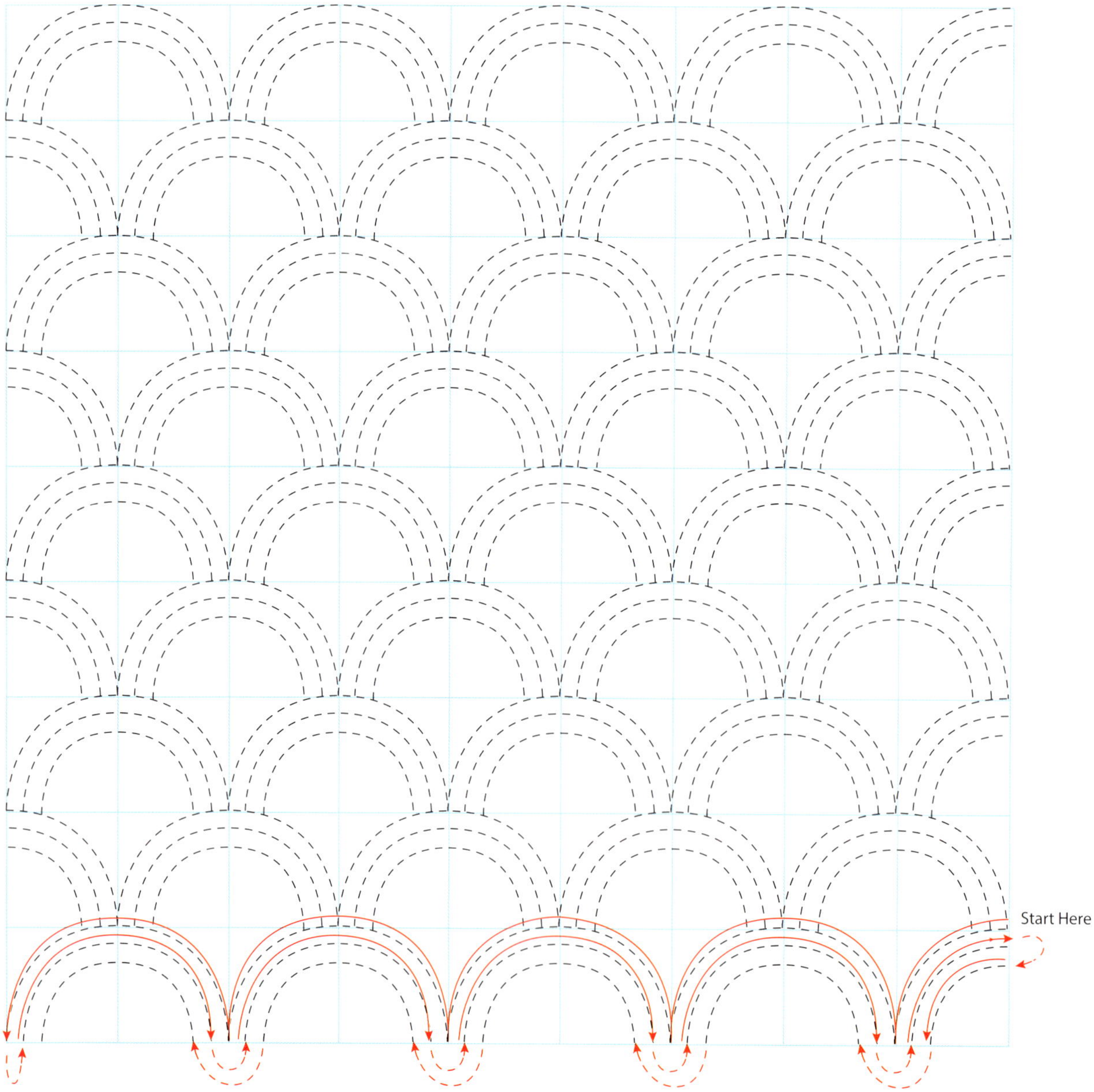

Start Here

Asanoha

Asanoha pattern is drawn on a 1:2 grid—for example, 1″ tall by 2″ wide (2.5 × 5.1cm).

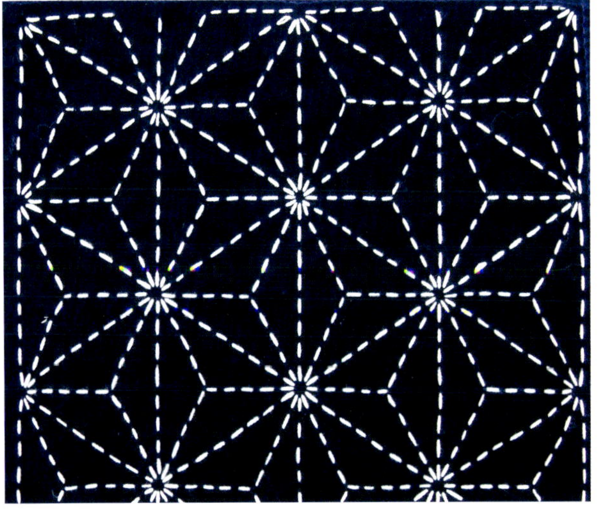

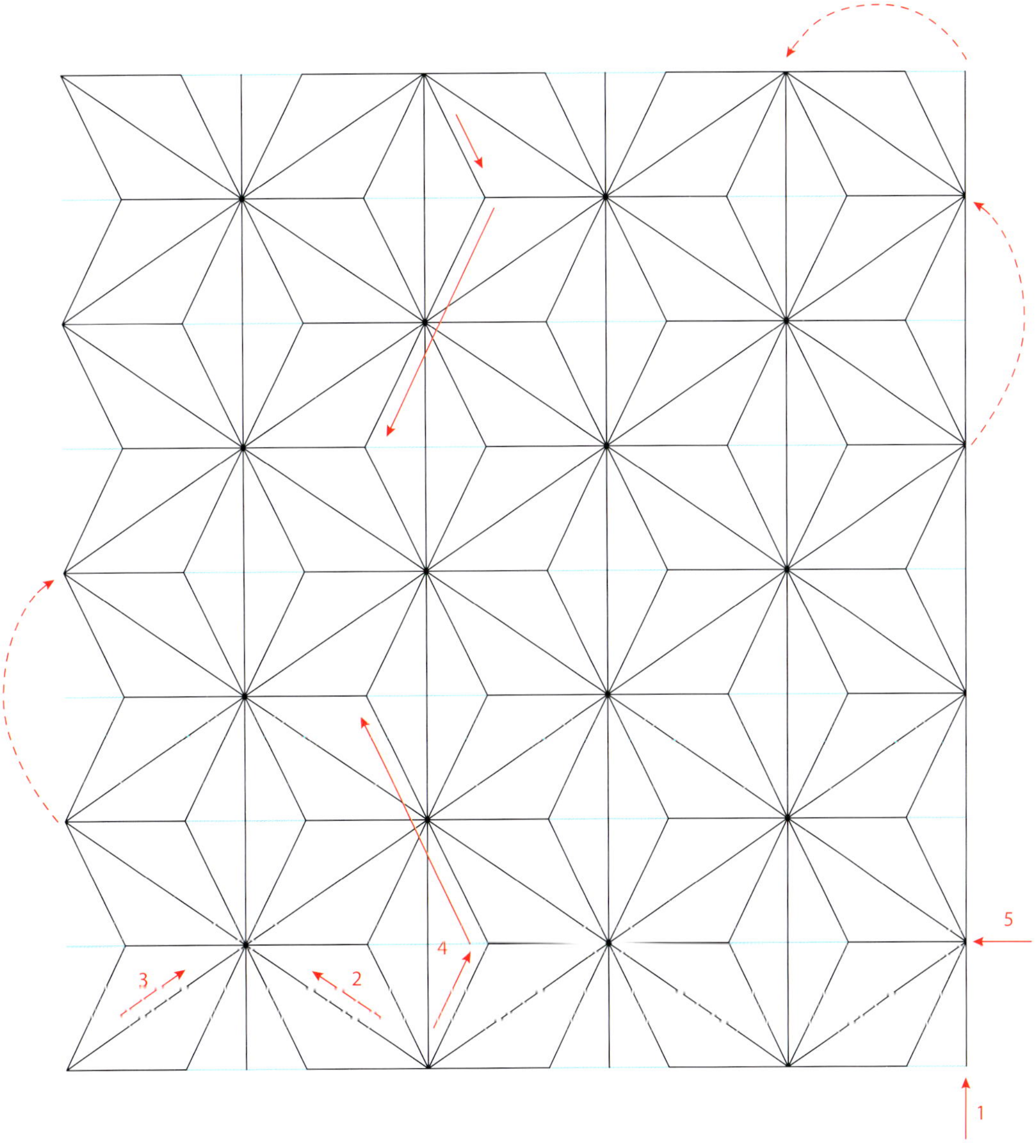

MARKING LINES FOR SASHIKO

Sashiko is a very particular creature in that it is nearly impossible to do without a pre-drawn grid or pattern lines. Simple offset running stitches can be done visually as is true with offset crosses, but even the most experienced sashiko stitcher will go a bit wonky at times, so it is best to mark those grids ahead of time for a more uniform look.

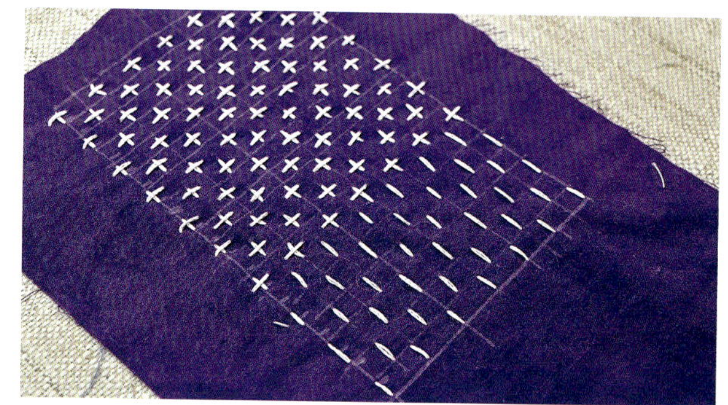

Hitomezashi Grid

For hitomezashi sashiko, the stitches are made on a 1:1 grid, meaning each grid space is the same length as the height. For most of our mending work, we use a ¼″ (6mm) grid, meaning each square is ¼″ × ¼″ (6 × 6mm).

1. Use a ruler or template to outline the area to be mended. We like to use see through quilting rulers whenever possible so we can see where the grid lines are going to cross on the mend. *fig. A*

2. Next, mark the outline with lines running one direction spaced ¼″ (6mm) apart. *fig. B*

3. Now mark lines spaced ¼″ (6mm) perpendicular to the first set of lines. *fig. C*

A.

B.

C.

Moyouzashi Grid

Moyouzashi sashiko patterns are drawn in two parts. The first is the grid and the second is the lines the pattern will be stitched on. In this book, we give dimensions of the grid, as well as the stitching lines for each pattern.

Draw the grid as indicated for the stitch pattern. In this example, we are using a 1″ × 2″ (2.5 × 5.1cm) grid for Diamonds (see page 87).

1. Draw a 1″ × 2″ (2.5 × 5.1cm) grid using a ruler or template. *fig. A*
2. Draw the stitching lines with a ruler or template being careful to follow the pattern given. Start with all of the diagonal lines running in one direction. *fig. B*
3. Then draw the diagonal lines running in the other direction. *fig. C*
4. Fill in any additional vertical or partial lines as needed for the pattern being stitched.

For circular moyouzashi patterns, such as blue ocean waves, we use a plastic drafting template to draw the half-circles onto the grid. *fig. D*

Generally, the more complex the stitch pattern, the more additional lines are required, so following the base grid and counting lines carefully when drawing the patterns is vital. Asanoha (page 89) is a prime example of this. It might seem complex to draw but taking it a step at a time pays off in a big way with a gorgeous stitch pattern.

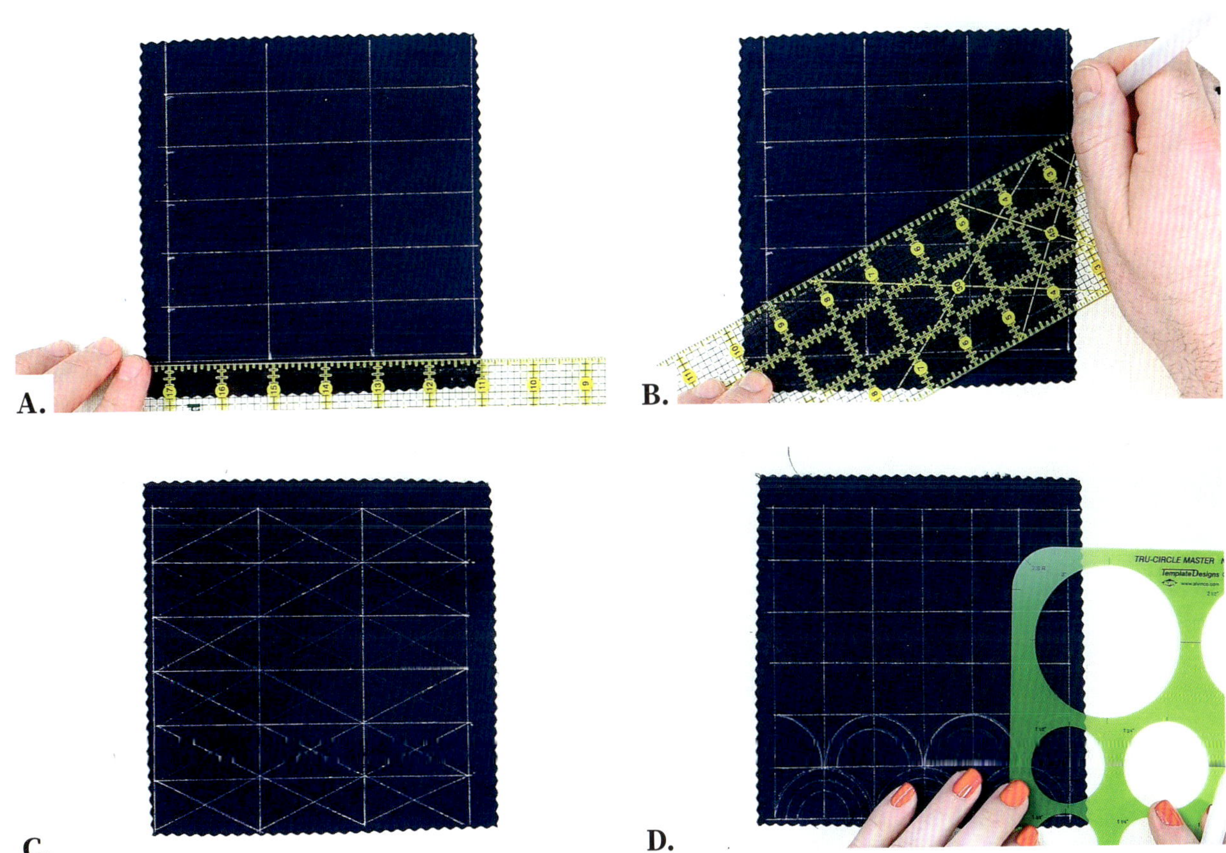

A. B. C. D.

UNSHIN: HANDLING THE NEEDLE

Sashiko running stitches are made without the assistance of a hoop so the fabric is hand tensioned. The stitches are made by loading fabric onto a long, sharp needle. The sashiko palm thimble is then used to push the needle through the gathered fabric, and the fabric is pulled over the length of thread. This takes a little practice, but the sashiko running stitch has replaced regular running stitches for us for everything from quilting and mending to sewing fabric together.

1. Coming from the back of the fabric, pull thread through leaving about ¼" (6mm) tail before the knot. *fig. A*
2. Brace the end of the sashiko needle with the eye against the palm thimble, using the little dimples in the metal to secure the end of the needle and keep it from slipping around. *fig. B*
3. Place your middle finger under the needle beneath the fabric. *fig. C*
4. Place your thumb on the top of the needle over the fabric. You now have the needle braced in three places. *fig. D*

A.

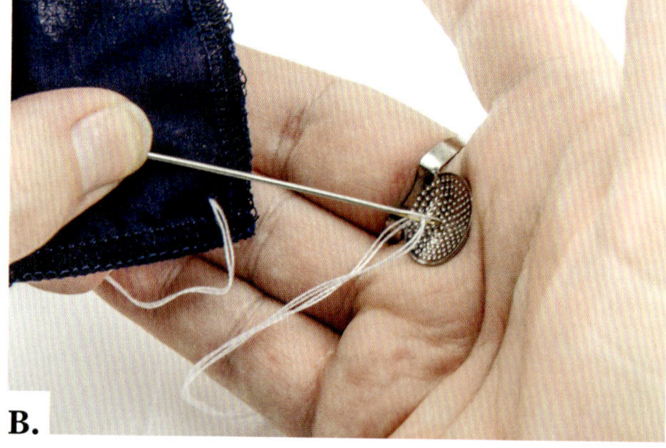

B.

C.

D.

The eye of the sashiko needle braced against the dimples of the palm thimble with thumb and middle finger pinching needle to fabric

5. Gather the fabric with your opposite hand. *fig. E*

6. With your needle hand, rock the needle down so the tip is below the fabric and gently push the needle forward with the palm thimble. You will use a very small movement with your fabric hand to lift the fabric slightly to meet the tip of the needle. *fig. F*

7. With your needle hand, rock the needle up so the tip is above the fabric, and continue to gently push the needle forward with the palm thimble. Use a very small movement with your fabric hand to push the fabric down slightly to meet the tip of the needle. *fig. G*

8. Continue to rock the needle up and then down as in Steps 6 and 7, moving the needle across the fabric and loading more fabric onto your needle. *fig. H*

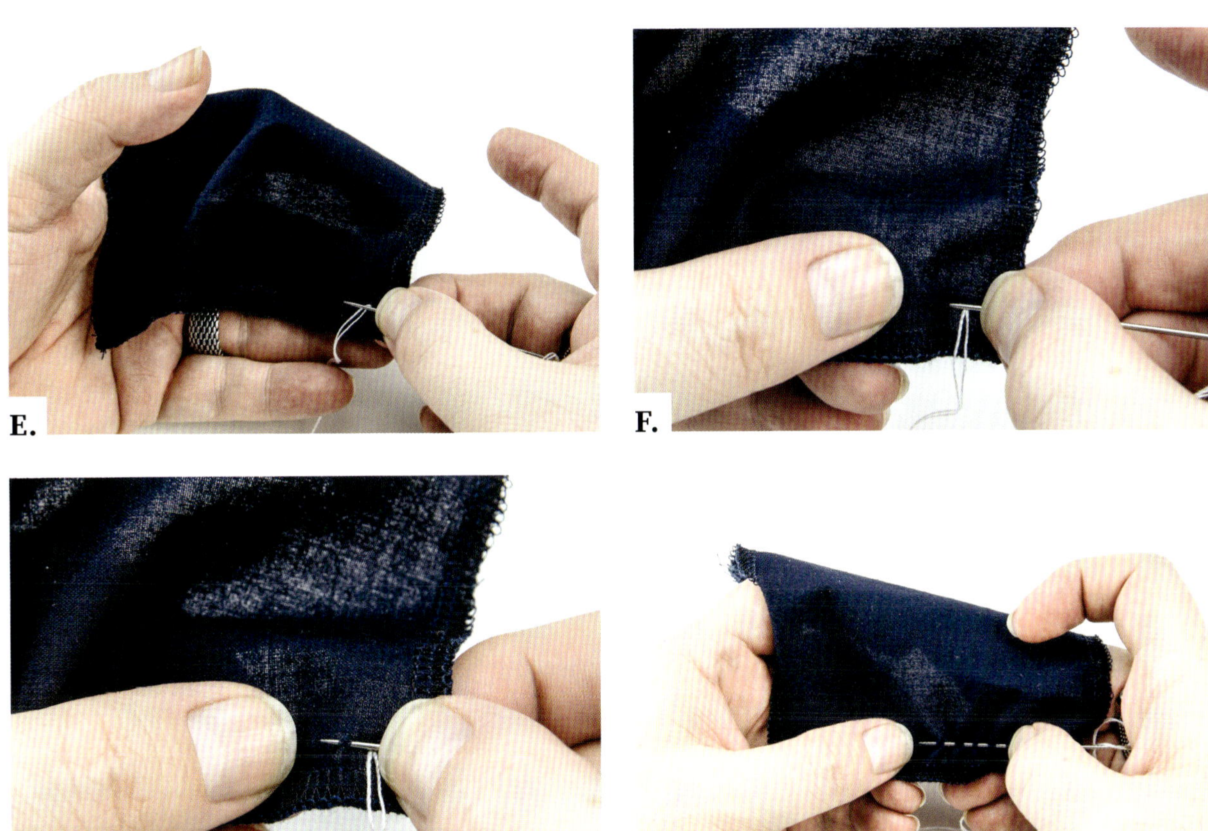

9. When you come to the end of your row (or the end of your fabric), finish your line of stitches with your needle point under the fabric. Remember to leave about ¼″ to ½″ (6–12mm) of unworked fabric at the edges of your swatch. Do not run your stitches right up to the edge of the swatch, or the fabric will tend to pucker and pull too easily. *fig. I*

10. Brace your needle against the palm thimble and hold the gathered fabric nearest the tip of the needle in place with the thumb and middle finger of your fabric hand so it doesn't move with the needle. Make sure your grip is firm enough to hold the fabric in place but loose enough to allow the needle to slide through your fingers. With the palm thimble, push the needle as far as possible through the gathered fabric. *fig. J*

11. Grab the gathered fabric again with your fabric hand by pinching the gathered fabric against the needle at the point where the needle tip comes out of the fabric. This will keep the gathered fabric from exploding off the tip of the needle. *fig. K*

12. With your needle hand, pull the fabric across the length of the thread while securely holding the needle with your fabric hand. *fig. L*

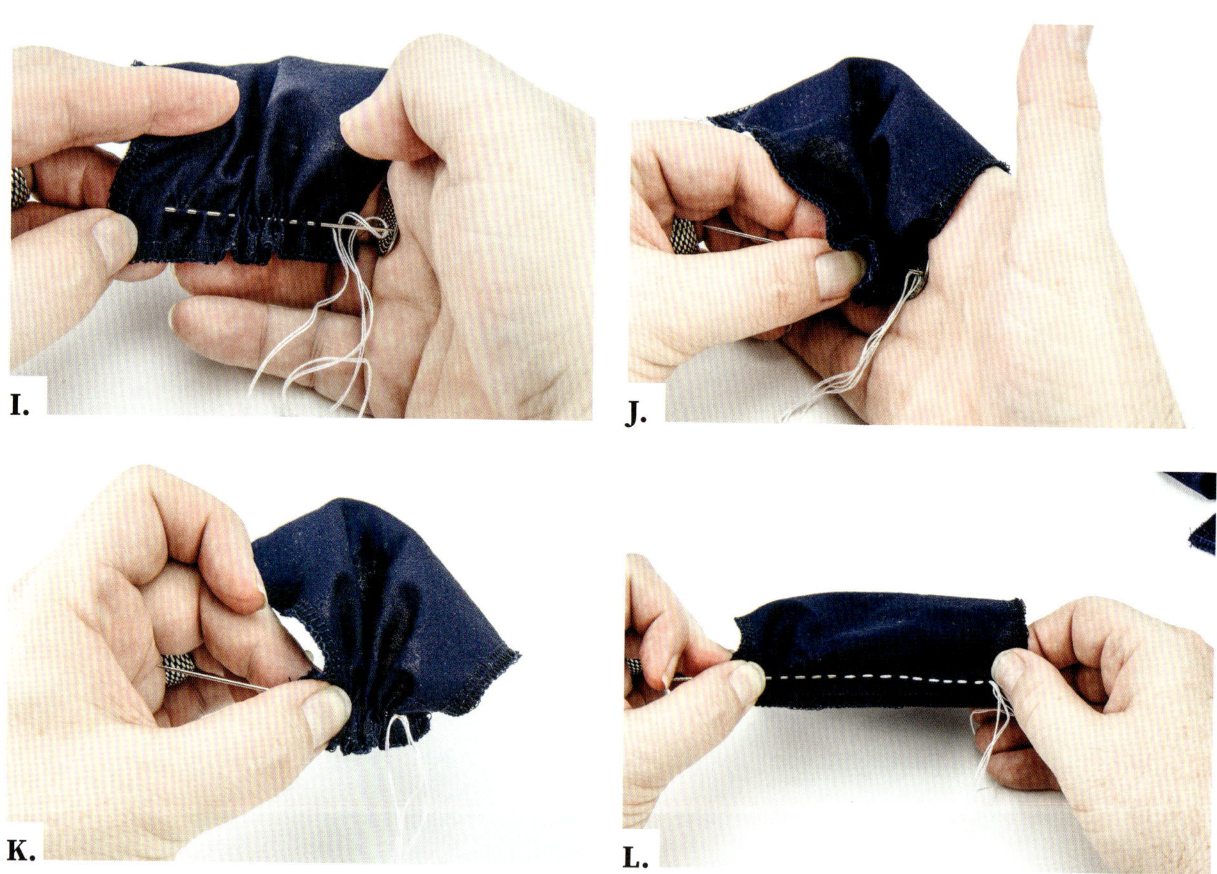

I.

J.

K.

L.

13. With your needle hand, pinch the fabric along with the knot end of the thread and gently run your fabric hand along the length of the thread (from the knot end to the needle end) to redistribute the fabric evenly. *fig. M*

14. While still pinching the fabric and knot end of the thread, give the fabric at the end of the row a gentle pull with your fabric hand to give a final check for evening out the stitches. This should cause a number of the stitches to pop up on the surface of the fabric. *fig. N*

15. Now, still pinching the fabric and knot end of the thread with your fabric hand, gently pull on the needle end of the thread until the stitches even out and lay neatly along the length of the fabric. Your goal is to have no stitches popped up above the surface of the fabric. *fig. O*

First row made …TA-DA!

M.

N.

O.

KNITS

Knits can be a particularly challenging mend because of the nature and construction of knit fabric. Snags are a less complex fix and can usually be done on the run whereas a run or a hole must be secured and attended to with some patience and time. Before beginning any mend on knits, be sure to prep the mend by following the steps in Knits Prep (page 19).

The properties of knit fabrics make them challenging when working the actual mend. Knit fabric moves freely in all directions and will stretch if hooped as for a mend on woven fabric. For this reason, we will often use a mending disk or the bottom of a jar to lay the fabric on, and then secure it with a rubber band. The key is to make sure the fabric lays snug to the surface without stretching. Stretching the fabric will cause the mend to be warped, and the stitches will not lay nicely when the fabric is relaxed.

Knit fabric is made in rows from a series of loops that are pulled through the previous row of loops. Stitches are made back and forth in horizontal rows picking up stitches through the loops of each row previously made. Thus, each row is dependent on the row above and below it, as well as the vertical columns of stitches on each side of the individual stitches. This means a hole in knit fabric will result in the stitches unraveling and creating a "run" that travels vertically. This panic-inducing type of mending event is not the end of the world ... although it might seem like it at first. Let's start with this fix first.

RUN

Discovering a run in a favorite piece of knitwear can cause reactions as small as a shoulder shrug and as severe as a toss into the bin. In most cases, the situation is not that dire and requires a little bit of patience to fix your beloved garment. The solution is to grab a crochet hook and loop those stitches back up the ladders (the horizontal lines of yarn left empty by the retreating stitches) of the run one at a time until all of the lone yarn is secured. A final set of duplicate stitches will ensure that the run is stable and secure.

1. Find the bottom of the run. This will be where the knit fabric is solid again and can be identified by following the horizontal lines of the unlooped stitches to the bottom until you find a live loop. Place a stitch marker or a safety pin in the live loop. *fig. A*

2. Now go to the top of the run and look for the cause of this near catastrophe. What you will find is a broken yarn that caused the first stitch to come undone and to run away down the column of stitches. *fig. B*

3. For any broken yarns, see Knits Prep (page 19).

A.

B.

4. Holding the fabric in hand, remove the stitch marker. Catch the live loop with the crochet hook and lift the loop up slightly while hooking the first unsecured horizontal yarn above the live loop. *fig. C*

5. Pull the horizontal yarn through the loop on the hook. *fig. D*

6. Gently lift the loop on the hook and use the crochet hook to grab the next unsecured horizontal yarn above the loop just made and pull through the loop on the hook. *fig. E*

7. Continue to lift loops and pull through loose horizontal yarn until the entire vertical line of stitches is secured. Place a stitch marker or safety pin in this last live loop and remove the hook.

8. Now, working from side to side and following the line where the broken thread was, work a single row of duplicate stitch (see Swiss Darning/Duplicate Stitch, page 108). *fig. F*

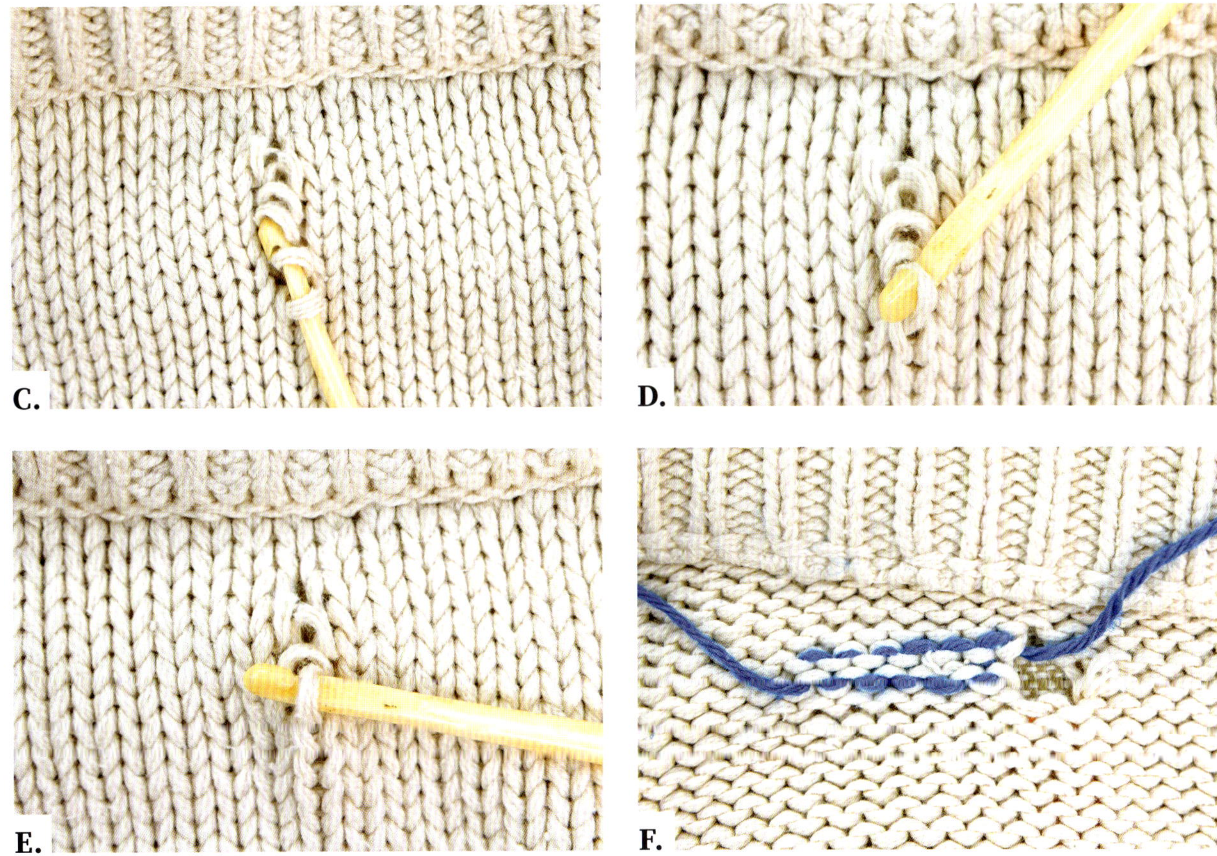

C. D. E. F.

9. Pick up the live stitch being held on a stitch marker by inserting the needle from back to front. *fig. G*

10. Now pass the needle behind the vertical bars of the stitch above the live stitch. *fig. H*

11. Bring the needle back down and through the live stitch from front to back. *fig. I*

12. Continue to work duplicate stitch, picking up live stitches along the row until the mend is complete. *fig. J*

Gently shape the yarn with your hands. Use a garment steamer if necessary to soften the yarn, gently pull the stitches into shape with a crochet hook and your hands, and lay the mended fabric flat.

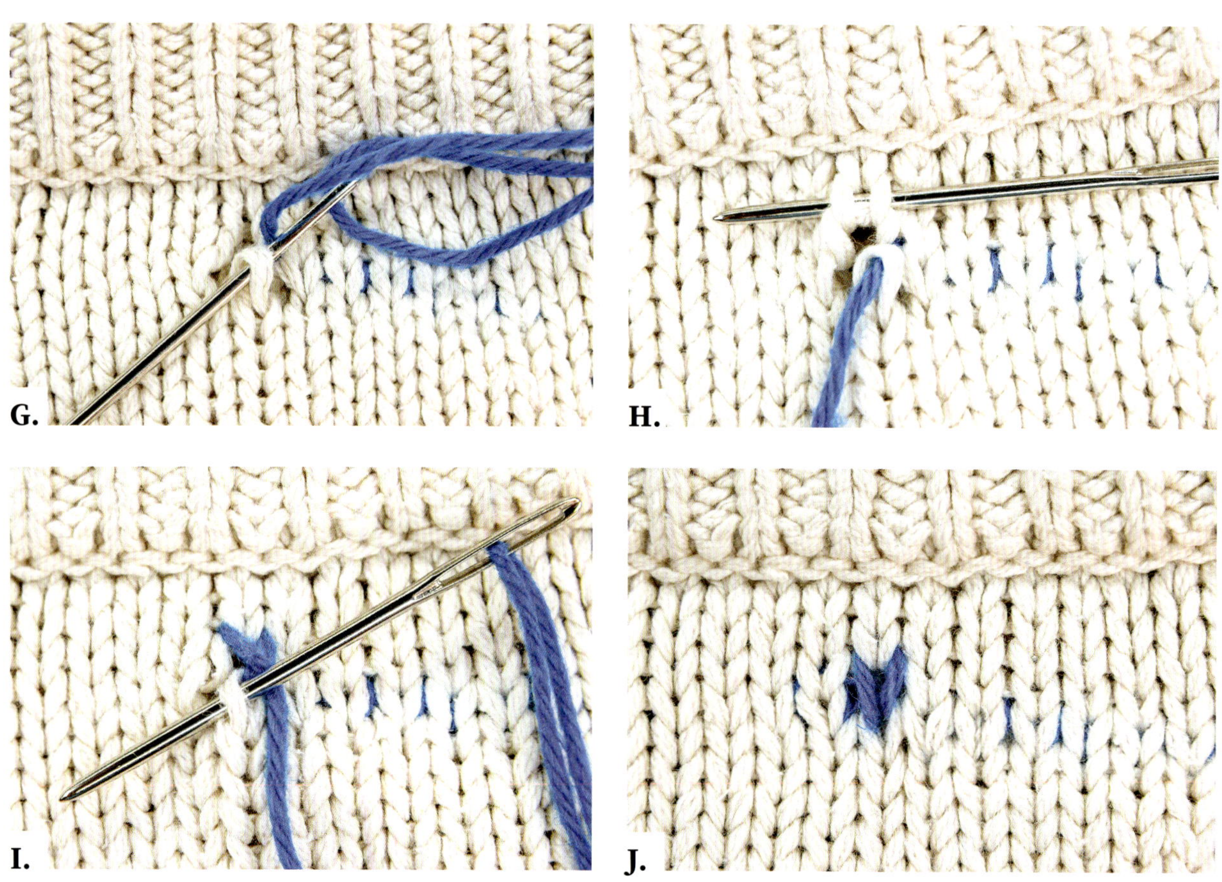

SNAGGED!

Another type of mend often required for knits is the dreaded snag. Fortunately, this is even easier to fix than the others. Most likely, the snag has stretched out only a single stitch without causing a broken yarn. Gently pulling the fabric from side to side and then top to bottom can coax the length of yarn back into place. If the loosened yarn will not go gently back from whence it came, grab that crochet hook and get to work.

1. Bring the crochet hook from back to front directly behind the snag and hook the offending snag with the crochet hook. *fig. A*

2. Gently pull the snag through to the back of the fabric. Once the snag is on the back of the fabric, gently pull the fabric in all directions to ensure that the mend will not be too tight and cause a pucker in the fabric. *fig. B*

3. Working from the back of the fabric, gently tie a knot in any excess yarn. If needed, use a little permanent fabric glue to secure any loose yarn. *fig. C*

4. Turn the fabric back to the front and observe the glory of your handiwork.

A.

C

B.

CEYLON STITCH

Also known as the faux knit stitch (okay, nobody else calls it that but that's how we've always referred to it, so here we are), this is an exciting surface design stitch when applied to woven fabric but is perfect for covering blemishes in knits. This stitch looks particularly good on woven fabric when worked in yarn.

1. Outline the mend with small backstitches (see page 30). The smaller the backstitches, the closer together the "knit" stitches will be. Make sure there are the same number of backstitches on the top and bottom of the mend and the same number on the left and right sides of the mend for an even look to the finished stitches. *fig. A*
2. Bring the needle up at the top corner through the hole below the first side stitch. *fig. B*
3. Pass the needle from top to bottom through the first horizontal backstitch. *fig. C*
4. Create a loop by passing the needle over the working yarn and gently tighten the loop. *fig. D*
5. Repeat Steps 3 and 4 across the row, ensuring the needle always passes over the working yarn. Be sure each loop is the same tension and size to ensure a uniform pattern. Adjust tension as needed. *fig. E*
6. At the end of the row, insert the needle back into the fabric at the hole below the side stitch that corresponds to the opposite end of the row. *fig. F*

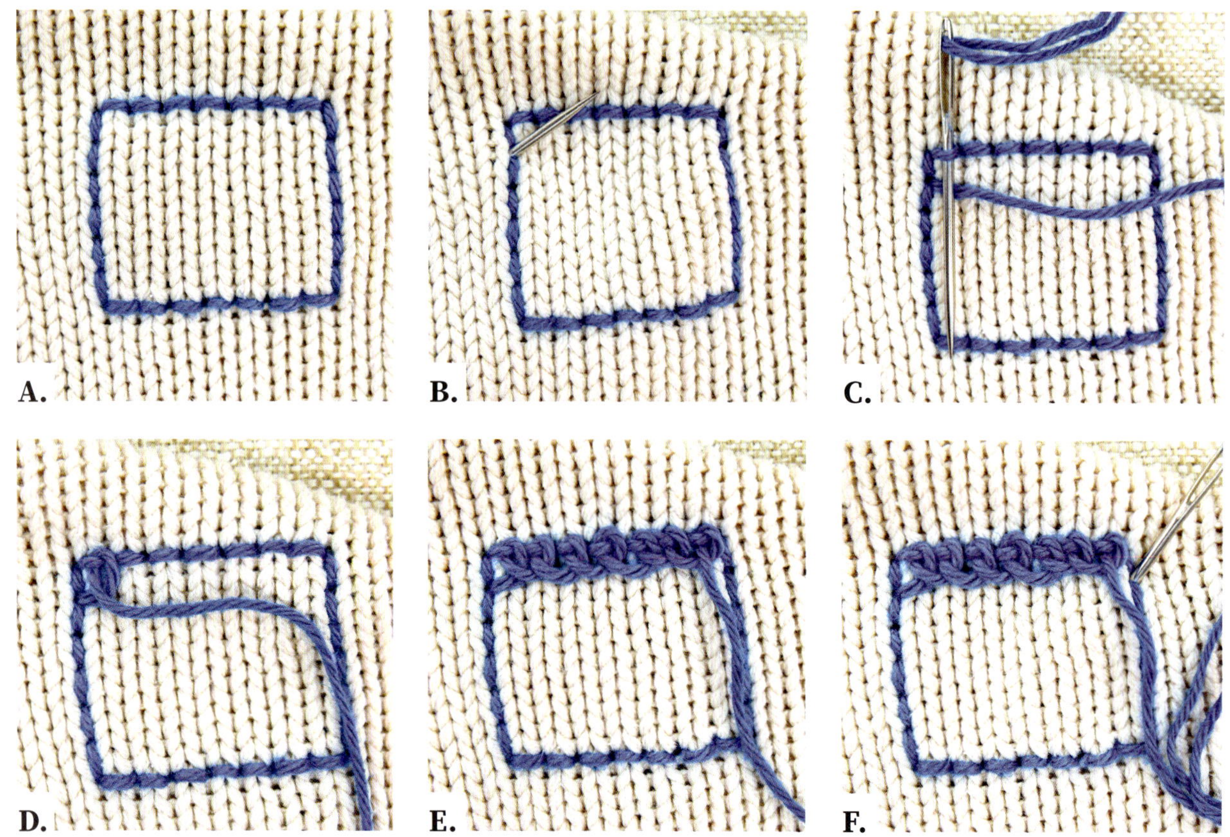

7. Bring the needle up at the bottom of the next stitch on the first side of the mend. *fig. G*

8. For this row, create loops by passing the needle behind the crossed threads of the loops of the previous row. *fig. H*

9. Continue in this manner until the final row. *fig. I*

10. For the final row, bring the needle up at the start of the row and create the loop as before. Now insert the needle from top to bottom into the bottom row of horizontal backstitches to anchor the floating stitches. *fig. J*

11. Continue to make anchored loops in this manner to the end of the row. At the end of the row, insert the needle into the end of the last horizontal backstitch. *fig. K*

12. Adjust any uneven stitches as needed. If using yarn, steam the yarn and allow it to set until dry to set the stitches. *fig. L*

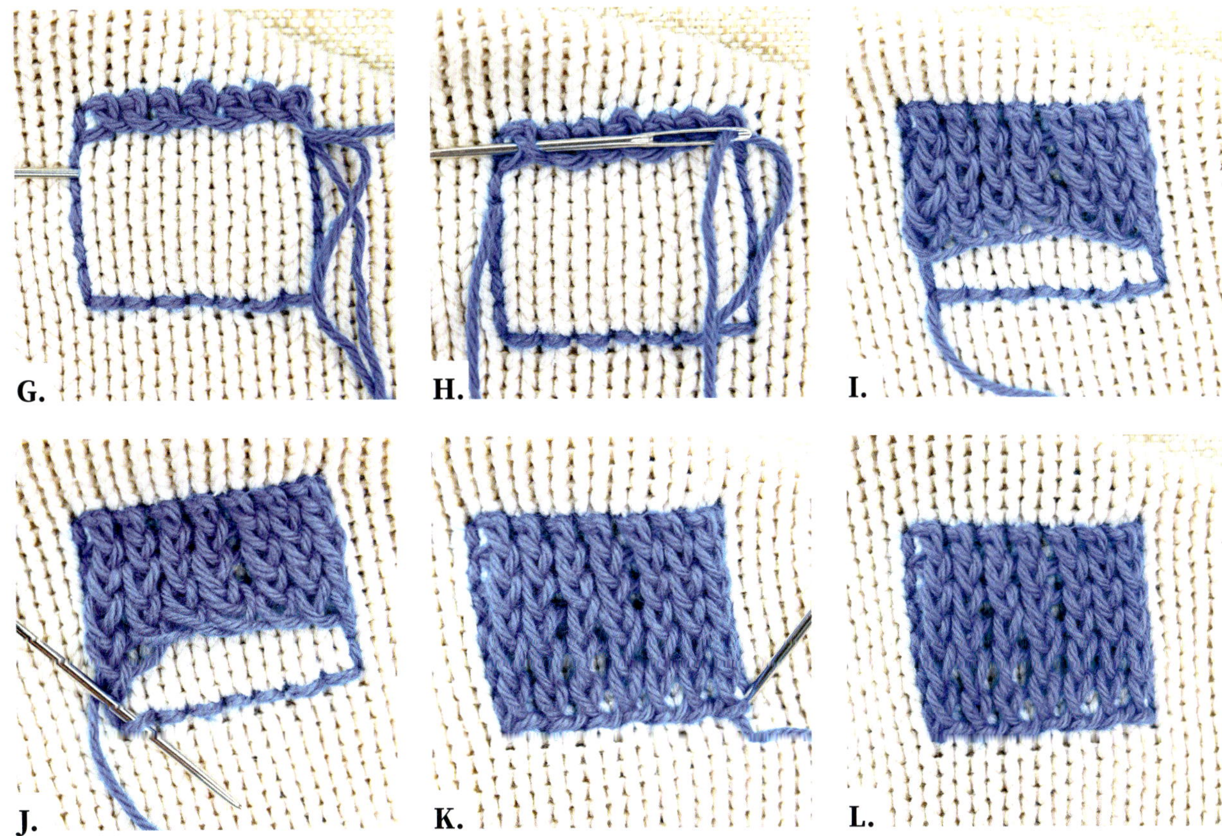
G. H. I. J. K. L.

SCOTCH DARNING

The elbows of much-loved sweaters and the heels of boot-worn woolen socks is where Scotch darning can most often be found. The dense stitching makes this mend secure and strong, ensuring that your favorite cardigan will live to see another season. Pay particular attention to the tension of the fabric being mended, as well as the tension of the stitches, to prevent puckering or loose stitches. Depending on the density and rigidity of the fabric, a darning egg or similar tool might come in handy here rather than a hoop.

Use stitch markers to secure any active loops, to prevent creating a run.

1. To begin, make running stitches (page 28) above the mend area along the top and extending about the same distance on either side of the mend. Leave a long tail at the start of the mending yarn. End with the needle and yarn on the front side of the fabric. *fig. A*

2. Now make a row of closely made blanket stitches (page 55) by bringing the needle down through the fabric following the line of running stitches just made. Pick up any live loops with the mending yarn. The closer together the stitches are, the more dense the new fabric will be and the stronger the mend. Be sure not to pull the stitches too tightly, or puckering will occur. *fig. B*

3. Continue making blanket stitches to the end of the row. Pass the needle through the main fabric to create the last few stitches. Finish the row with an anchor stitch. *fig. C*

4. To create the next row, bring the needle out 1 row below the row just made and make running stitches on the same side of the mend to the edge of the hole. *fig. D*

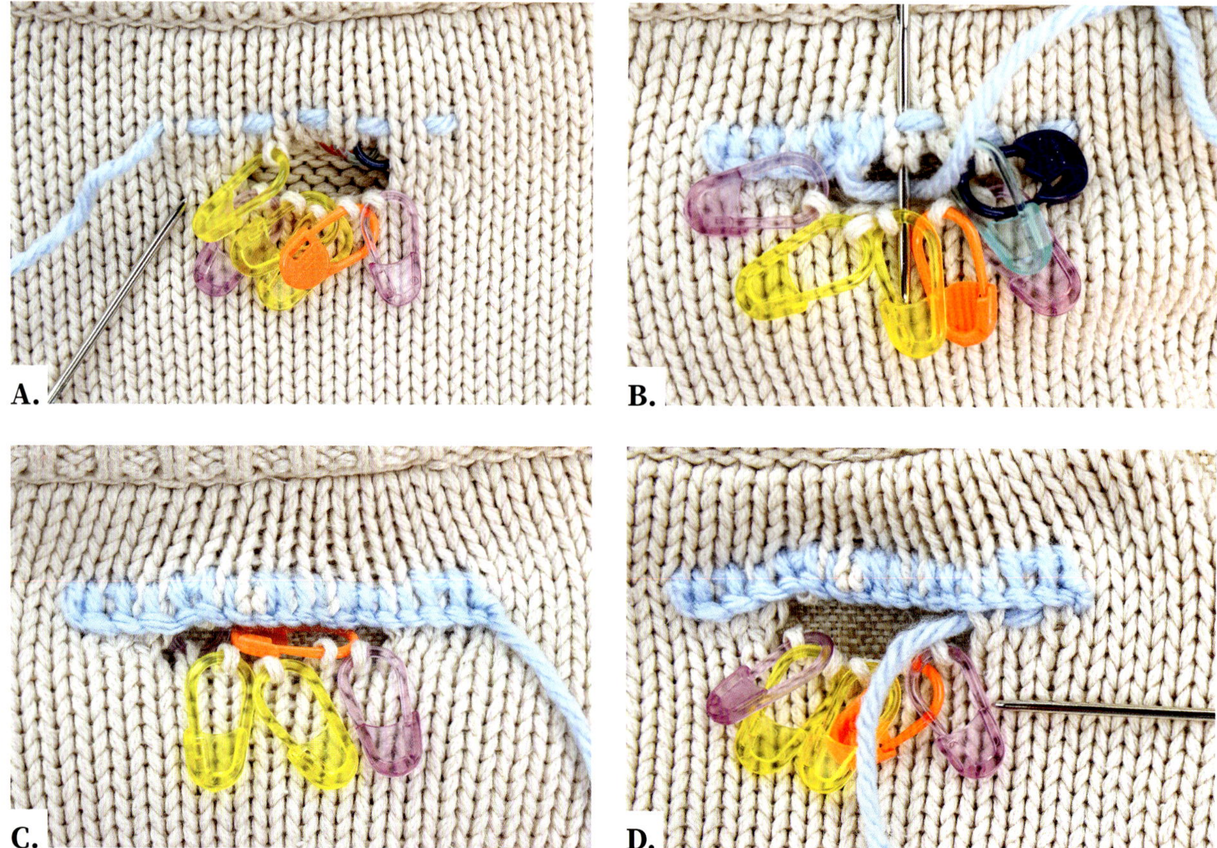

A. B. C. D.

5. String the yarn across the mend to the opposite side and make running stitches to secure. Be sure to keep the tension of this loose length of yarn (a float) consistent with the tension of the fabric. *fig. E*

6. Make a row of blanket stitches by passing the needle down through the horizontal bars of the previous row and behind the float before passing it through the new loop. *fig. F*

7. Continue in this manner to the end of the row and secure with an anchor stitch. *fig. G*

8. Repeat Steps 2–8 to the last row at the bottom of the hole or damaged spot.

9. To set up this final row, make running stitches to the end of the hole and then pick up any live stitches. Finish the set up by making running stitches in the fabric on the opposite side of the hole. *fig. H*

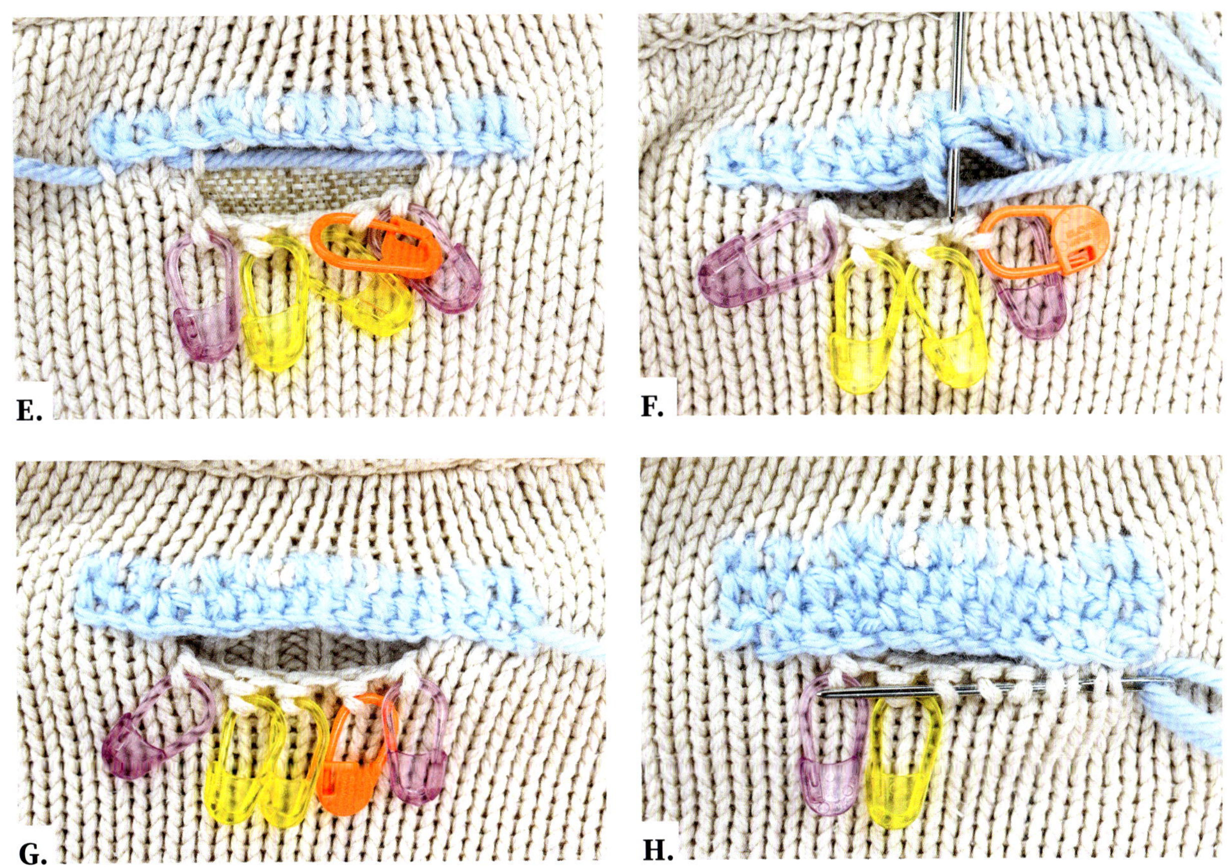

10. Make a row of connected blanket stitches, ensuring that the needle goes through the main fabric and the live stitches again to secure them. *fig. I*

11. Make one more row of running stitches below the mend area and cover with connected blanket stitches, as with the previous rows. *fig. J*

12. Weave in all of the yarn tails from the back of the work. *fig. K*

13. Steam the mend to smooth and flatten, adjusting the tension as needed.

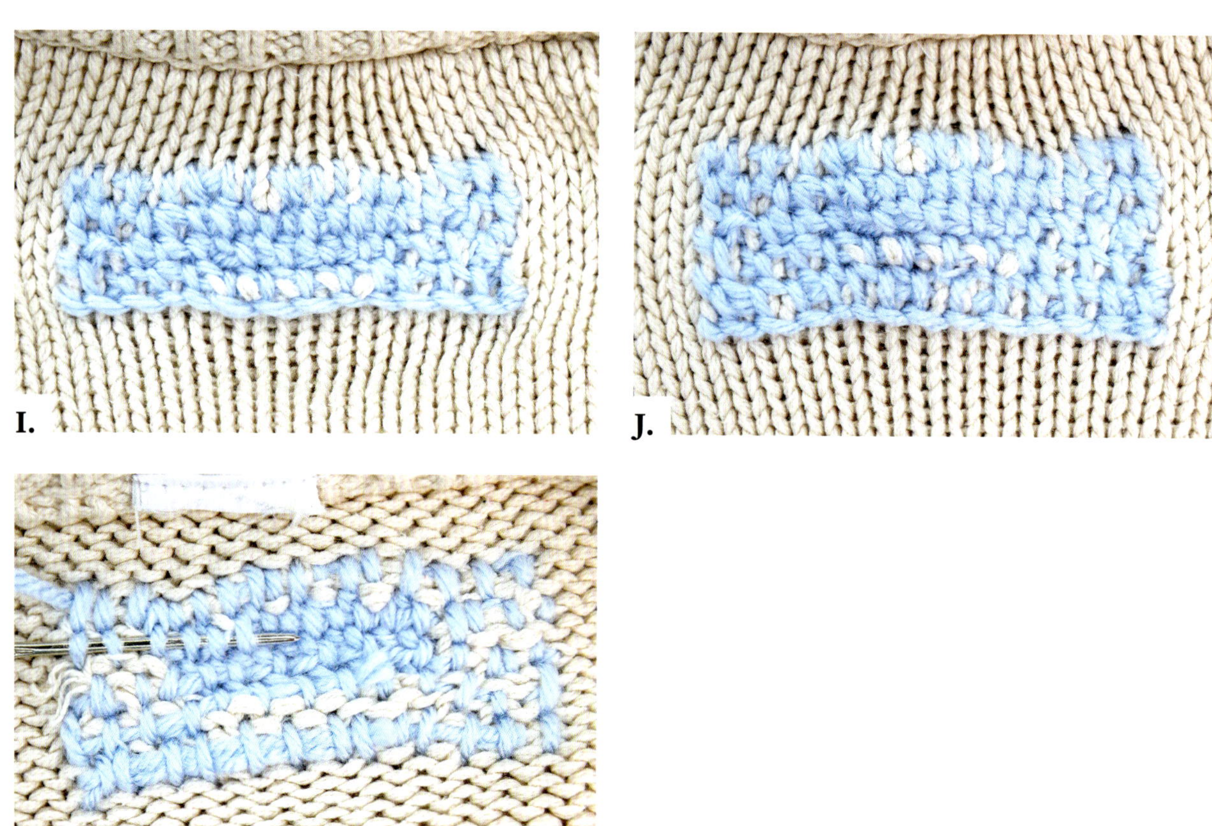

I. **J.** **K.**

WOVEN DARNING

Woven darning on knits is the same as on woven fabric, with the exception of the setup. As you work this patch, keep in mind that the tighter weave, the more secure the patch will be. See Weave Stitch (page 75) for additional information about this stitch.

1. Start 1 or 2 rows above and about 1″ (2.5cm) past the mend and make horizontal running stitches to the hole in the fabric. Finish with the needle behind the fabric and start the next row by bringing the needle up at the opposite end of the mend. *fig. A*

2. Float the yarn horizontally across the hole and secure to the opposite side with running stitches. *fig. B*

3. Repeat, working down the mend and past the bottom 1 or 2 rows. *fig. C*

4. Now working vertically, make running stitches along the outside edge of the mend, passing the needle over and then under the existing running stitches to create a woven pattern. *fig. D*

5. Pass the needle over and under the floats, alternating the previous stitches. If a stitch passed under on the previous row, this row will pass over. If a stitch passed over on the previous row, this row will pass under. Continue until the mend is filled. *fig. E*

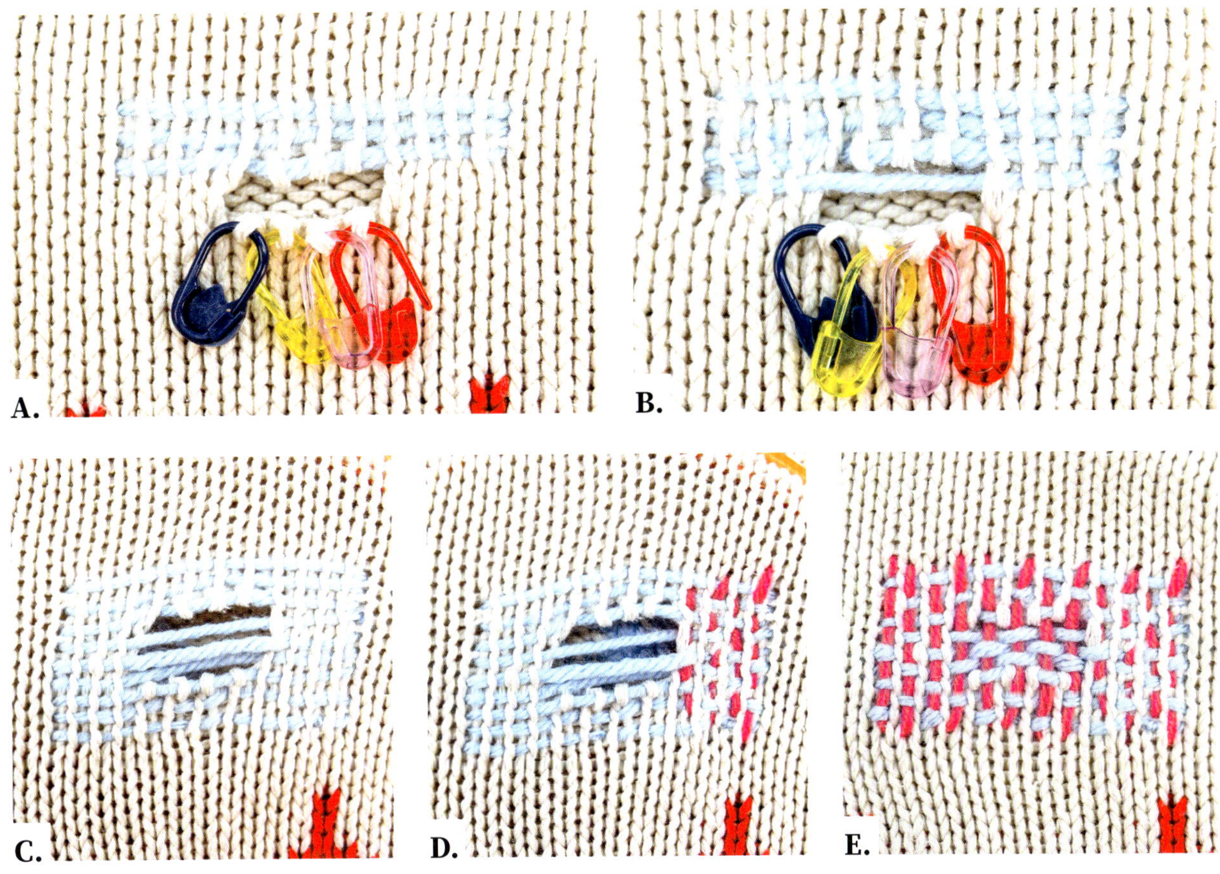

SWISS DARNING (DUPLICATE STITCH)

Swiss darning looks like the Ceylon stitch but is actually worked into the knit fabric rather than being a surface design stitch. Think of the duplicate stitch as the great multitasker of the knit fabric world. If a piece of knit fabric is showing signs of wear and some of the yarn is threatening to break (such as the elbow of a cardigan or the heel of a sock), a series of duplicate stitches will cover and reinforce those stitches. If there is a stain on a knit piece, the duplicate stitch can cover that stain beautifully with new yarn.

1. Starting approximately 2 rows below and outside the mend, bring the needle up through the center of a stitch and pass the needle under the vertical bars directly above. *fig. A*

2. Insert the needle back into the center of the stitch where it came from and out through the center of the neighboring stitching. *fig. B*

3. Pull the yarn taught to match the tension of the underlying knit fabric. First duplicate stitch made. *fig. C*

4. Pass the needle under the vertical bars of the new stitch and continue to the end of the row, making duplicate stitches 2 stitches beyond the mend area. End with the needle on the back of the fabric. *fig. D*

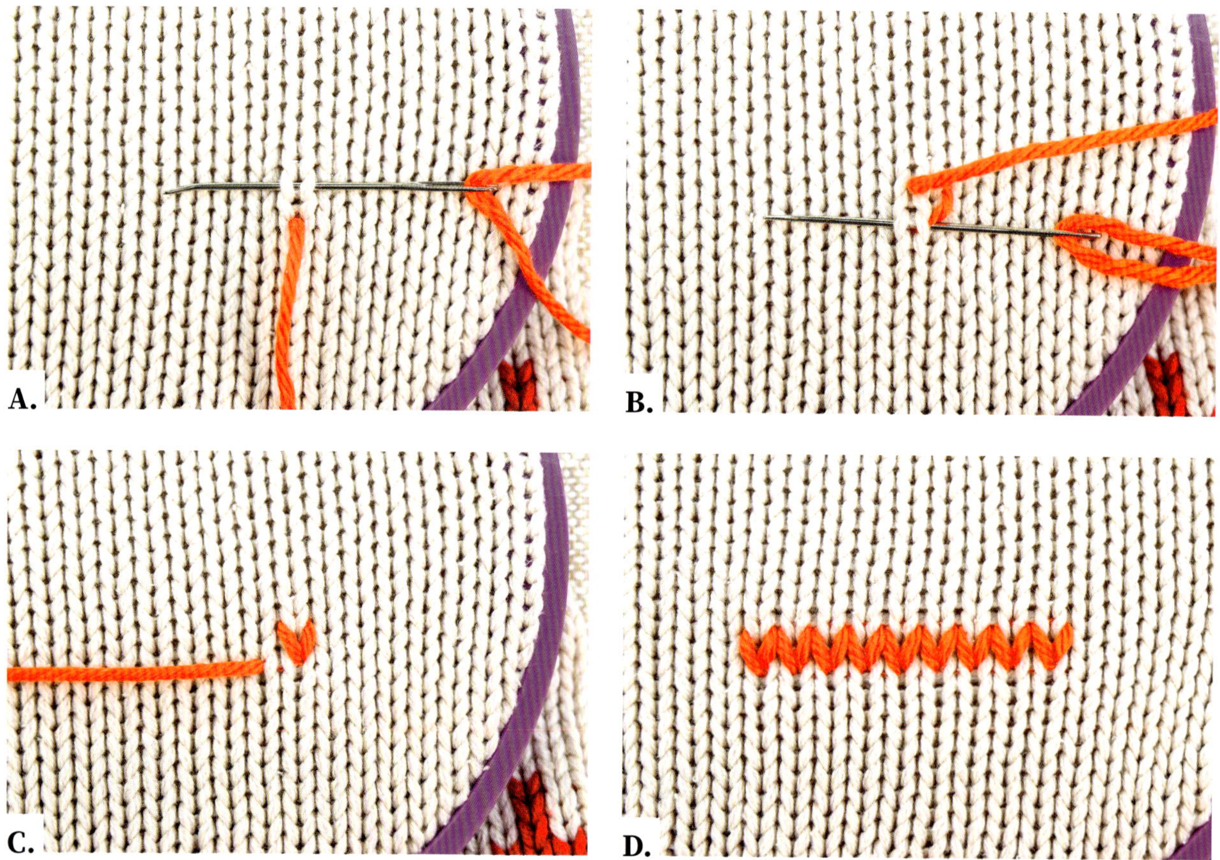

5. Bring the needle up through the center of the last duplicate stitch made. *fig. E*

6. Pass the needle under the vertical bars directly above. *fig. F*

7. Insert the needle back where it came from into the center of the stitch. *fig. G*

8. Continue to make a row of duplicate stitches on top of the first row. *fig. H*

Add rows of duplicate stitches one on top of the other until the mend is covered. Weave in yarn tails from the back of the work.

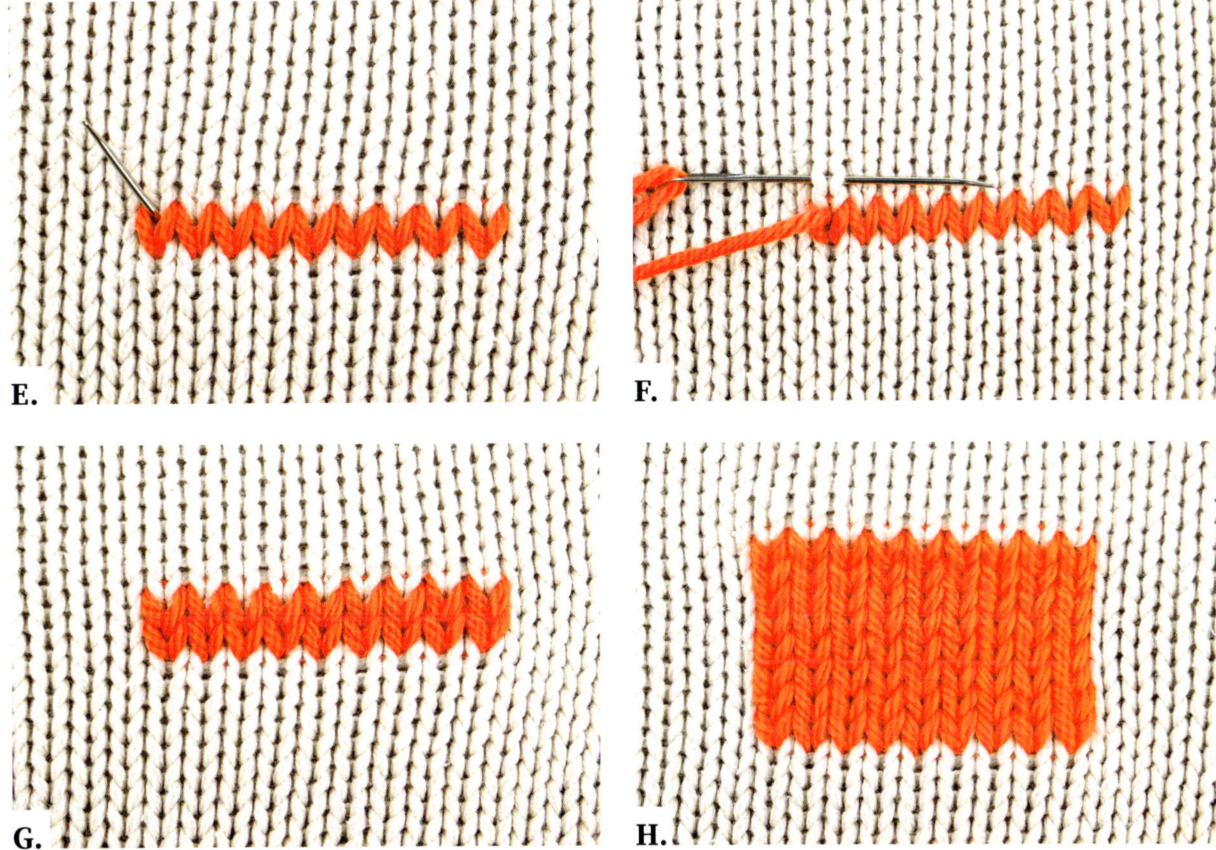

PATCH MENDING

Do you, like we do, remember the days of those iron-on patches that instantly hardened to a cement-board consistency upon cooling? They came in packs of colors from light to dark and were meant to blend in with the fabric they were patching and reinforcing. Unfortunately, they didn't exactly blend in, and the rigid, unyielding texture made them less than desirable to wear. And who can forget how they cracked and flaked off after a few washes, leaving a bigger mess than they fixed? Hand-stitched appliqué patches were better, but visible mending wasn't always as in fashion as it has become in recent years, and a quick fix meant the resulting mend was, often, rough at best. So, yeah ... while the sentiment of preserving our fabric for as long as possible is the same, let's explore some more aesthetically pleasing options than those iron-on and rough-stitched, make-it-work monsters.

There are two different purposes for patches: to reinforce a weak fabric or to cover or fill a hole or damaged area of fabric. When the fabric on the knee of a pair of well-loved jeans starts to show those telltale signs of thinning or when the cuff of your favorite Saturday comfy shirt starts to fray, a patch to reinforce the fabric before it gives way completely is a useful and potentially decorative preventive measure. If the seat of those hiking pants just could not stand up to the rigors of sliding down one too many trails and an unwanted ventilation hole opens up, a patch to cover the offending rend is just what is called for. In fact, combined with the right blend of reinforcing stitches, a patch can prolong the life of jackets, furniture textiles, jeans, shirts, and tees, bringing new life to aging or thrifted garments as wearable patchwork textile art pieces.

MAKE YOUR OWN PATCHES

The popularity of those aforementioned iron-on patches is easy to understand because they are a quick fix that doesn't require a lot of fuss. It is for that same reason that we like to keep a supply of patching fabric scraps and fusible products on hand to make quick patches when needed or even to make a few in advance to keep in a repair kit for emergencies.

All that is required are some small pieces of a favorite fabric—much like the fabric we inherited from Jason's mother, pink with flamingoes. (We are certain it was originally going to be a pair of wonderfully gaudy boxers for Jason.) Those flamingoes can now be found peeking out from worn knees and pocket edges on several mended garments. Other options are quilt blocks that didn't make the final cut or improv fabric that didn't fit in as intended. Yes, we also keep around a healthy supply of odd cuts of denim and other assorted fabrics scraps.

Be a Little Extra

Make a few more of these while you are in the process. One, they are fun to make, and two, extras are useful to have on hand for quick repairs when you don't have time for as much fun. Pop a couple into a travel repair kit for when that cabinet drawer grabs the seat of your slacks.

Whether using appliqué or iron-on methods for attaching a patch, preparing the patch ahead of time is the same. First, decide if the patch will have turned or raw edges.

If the edges are to be turned, fold the cut edges to the back side of the fabric, trim off the folded corners, and press. We like to use a little fabric basting glue to ensure the edges stay in place.

If the cut edges of the patch are to remain raw, decide if fraying is acceptable or if the edges should be secured with a fusible product. For example, with denim patches, we usually leave the edges raw and will even wash and dry them ahead of time to enhance the worn, frayed look.

If the patch fabric needs to be thicker to give added protection to the underlying mend, a stabilizer, or other fusible product can be added to give the patch fabric added strength.

Once the patch is created, the next decision is whether to appliqué or iron on. Of course, before starting any patch, see Woven Prep (page 17).

Appliqué Patches

Appliqué patches use a combination of fusible backing or basting glue to hold them on the mended fabric before adding edge stitches to secure them in place. First, create the turned edge or raw edge patch of your choice; then pick any one or more of the edge or filler stitches from the Stitch Index (page 22).

Iron-On Patches

Iron-on patches are similar to appliqué patches but can be used without the edge stitching to attach the patch to the mended fabric. Make the turned edge or raw edge patch you like best; then apply the double-sided fusible product to the back of the patch according to the manufacturer instructions. Once the fusible is cooled and set, the patch is ready to be applied or can be set aside for later use.

Next, let's take a look at the mend and decide on a top patch or an under patch.

TOP PATCHES

Top Iron-On Patches

1. Cut the patch fabric or create an iron-on patch a little larger than the mend area and matching double-sided fusible. We like to use a patch that is at least 1–2 inches (2.5–5.1cm) larger than the mend area. *fig. A*

2. To apply an iron-on patch, peel off the paper backing, lay the patch onto the mending area, and press with a hot iron. Check the edges of the patch to ensure that it is secured all the way around. Bonus: Use the paper backing as a shield between the glue from the patch and the pressing board. *fig. B*

3. Add any additional stitching around the edges of the patch to further secure or just because it looks good ... nothing wrong with that! *fig. C*

Top Appliqué Patches

To apply an applique patch, select an edge stitch or overall stitch from the Stitch Index (page 22), such as sashiko or a decorative embroidery stitch.

A.

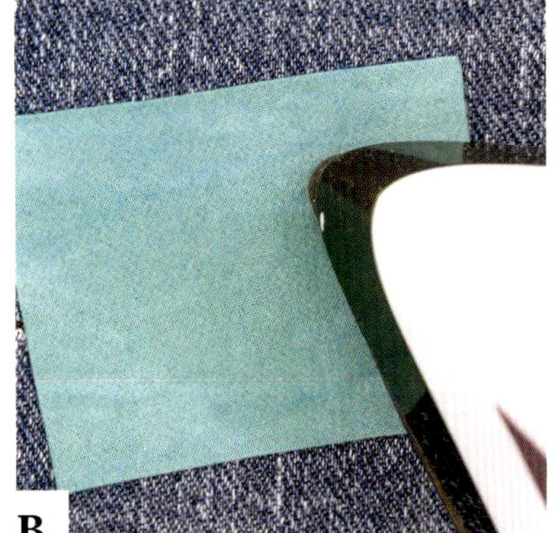

B.

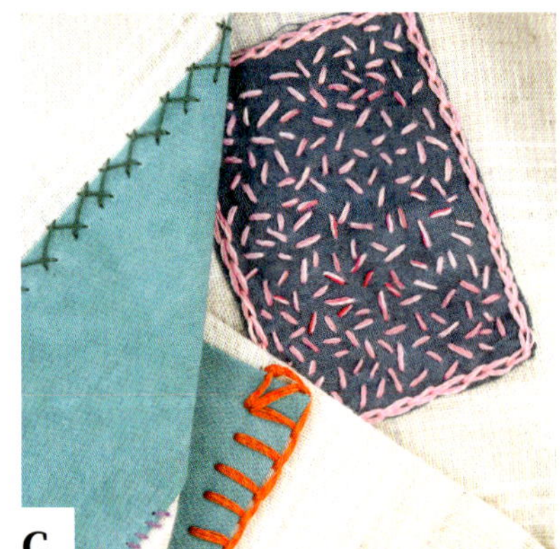

C.

UNDER PATCHES

1. Center the patch fabric behind the mend area. If the mend is a hole and you have a feature on the patch fabric that you want to show through the hole (such as this flower or Jason's flamingoes), make sure it is clearly visible. Have we increased the size of a hole before to show more of a flamingo or a face? Yes. Absolutely. *fig. A*

2. Use temporary basting glue or permanent fabric glue to secure the patch fabric behind the mend fabric. Scrap pieces of double-sided fusible can also be applied here as an alternative. Then, press the area with an iron to set the glue or fusible. *fig. B*

3. If you're making an overall stitch pattern to secure the patch, it is best to stitch about 1″ (2.5cm) past the patch on all sides. For this reason, use a heat-erasable or washable pen to outline the area of the patch. *fig. C*

4. Stitch through the mend fabric and the patch fabric with either an overall pattern or around the hole and the edge of the patch. Finish by erasing the marked lines with heat or wash. *fig. D*

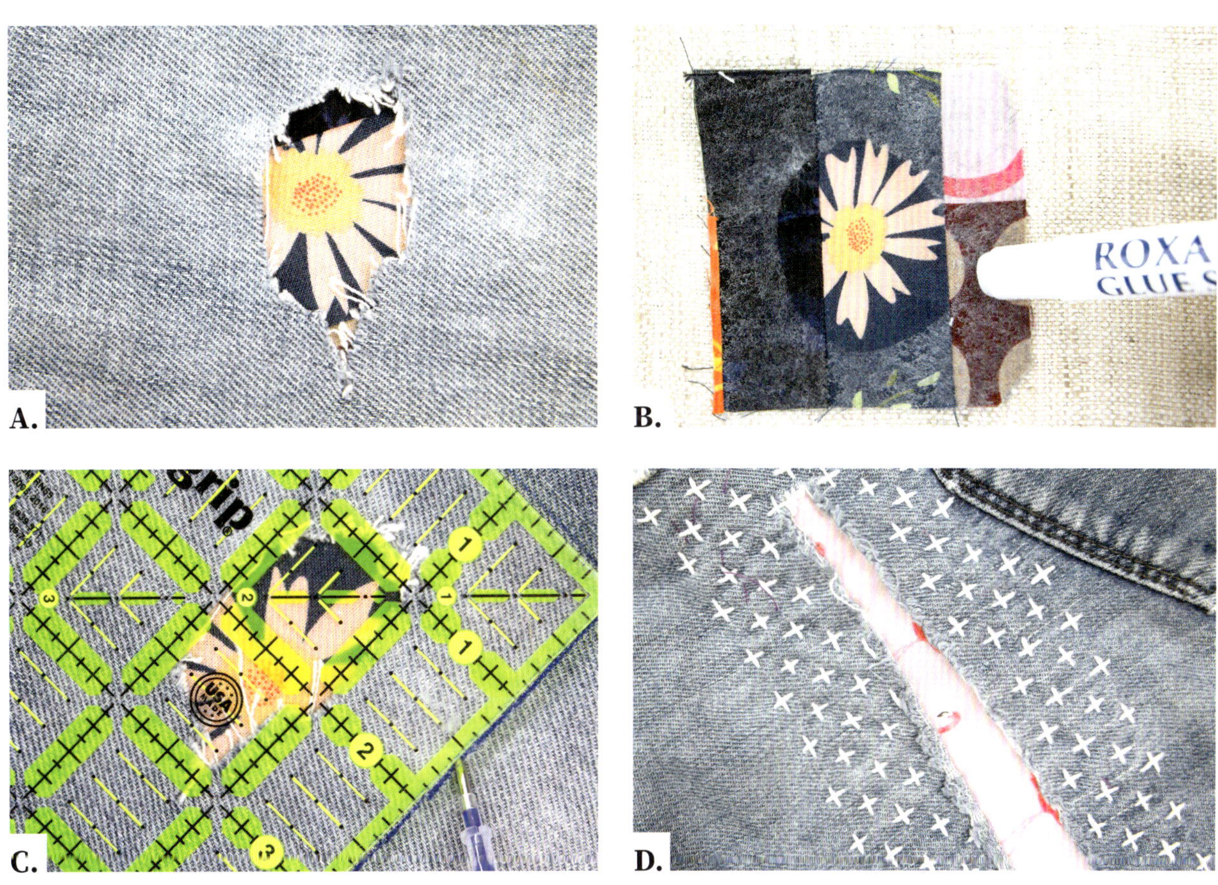

Note • Anything Goes

We make a lot of sashiko and embroidery step-outs for our workshops, and some of those turn into patches. We also have boxes of quilt blocks from our books and workshops that either didn't make the final cut or were an odd size or color and those make FAB embellishments and patches. And don't be afraid to be creative. Layer pieces of lace, home dec fabric, or crochet motifs with solid fabric to make patches. Why play it safe?

Boro Patches

Boro mending is a form of Japanese mending where fabric is added on top of damaged or worn fabric for the purposes of mending, reinforcing, and beautifying. The boro patch fabric, with either raw or turned edges, similar to other appliqué patches, is top-stitched into place with bordering running stitches or with an overall stitch pattern to secure the patch (see Sashiko, page 80). Often, we take these boro patches to the extreme and use them to completely cover fabric that is not to our liking anymore or that has become so worn that it is no longer suitable for public presentation. The result is a brand-new garment that can be enjoyed for many more years.

Note • Deeper Dive

For a deeper dive into boro and sashiko fabric, be sure to check out our book Boro and Sashiko: Harmonious Imperfection, *from C&T Publishing.*

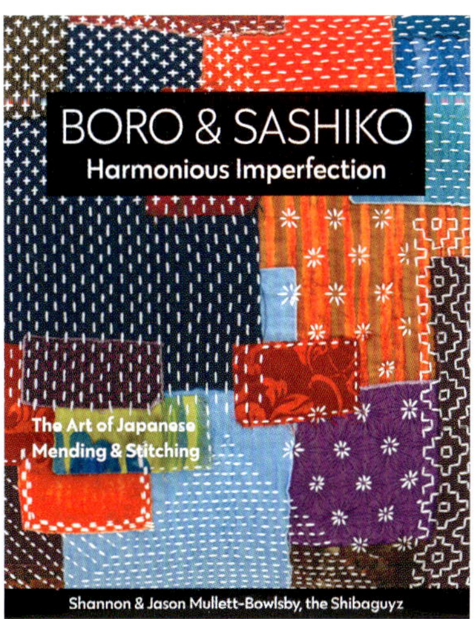

QUICK FIXES

Quick fixes encompass buttons, hems, emergency repairs, and no-sew fixes.

Not all fixes need to be permanent. Sometimes we just need that hem to stay in place for a few hours longer until we have time to sit down with our mending kit and give it the attention it deserves. And that vicious desk drawer that reached out and tore a hole in the seat of your favorite trousers does deserve a good swift kick, but first let's patch up that rip so it doesn't become a NSFW moment.

ATTACHING BUTTONS

If the button fell off or broke, the original thread holes are probably still visible. If that is the case, use those holes as a guide for attaching the new button.

1. If the button is gone and the original stitching holes are no longer visible, lay the garment flat and overlap the buttonhole on top of the spot where the button should be.

2. Use an erasable pen to mark the spot where the new button will be attached.

3. Use a small marking tool or pins to mark the new stitching holes so the button is attached straight.

Attach a Flat Button

1. Thread your needle with a doubled strand of heavyweight button thread. Bring the needle up from the back to the front through one of the stitching holes or marked stitching spots. *fig. A*

2. Make a tack stitch in this same spot to secure the thread. A tack stitch is made by making a few small stitches over 2 or 3 threads all in the same place. *fig. B*

3. Now bring the needle up through 1 hole of the button. *fig. C*

4. Insert the needle back through the next buttonhole. *fig. D*

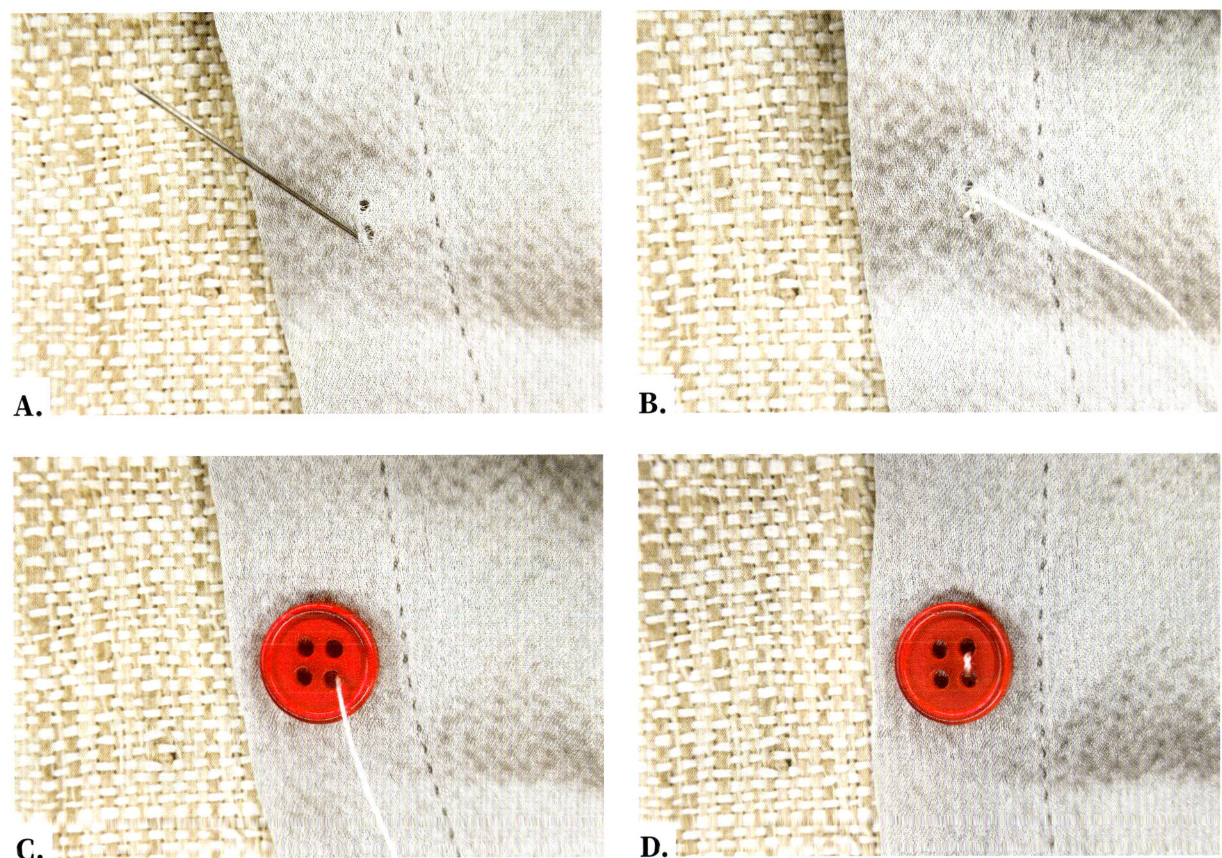

A. B. C. D.

5. Insert the needle into the corresponding stitching hole in the fabric. Snug the stitch just made, but do not tighten it too much. *fig. E*

6. Continue to work up and over the holes in the button several times until the button is secure. *fig. F*

7. Insert the needle through the last buttonhole and through the back of the fabric. Make a small tack stitch on the back of the fabric. *fig. G*

8. Make a knot, bury the thread tail in the fabric, and trim it off. *fig. H*

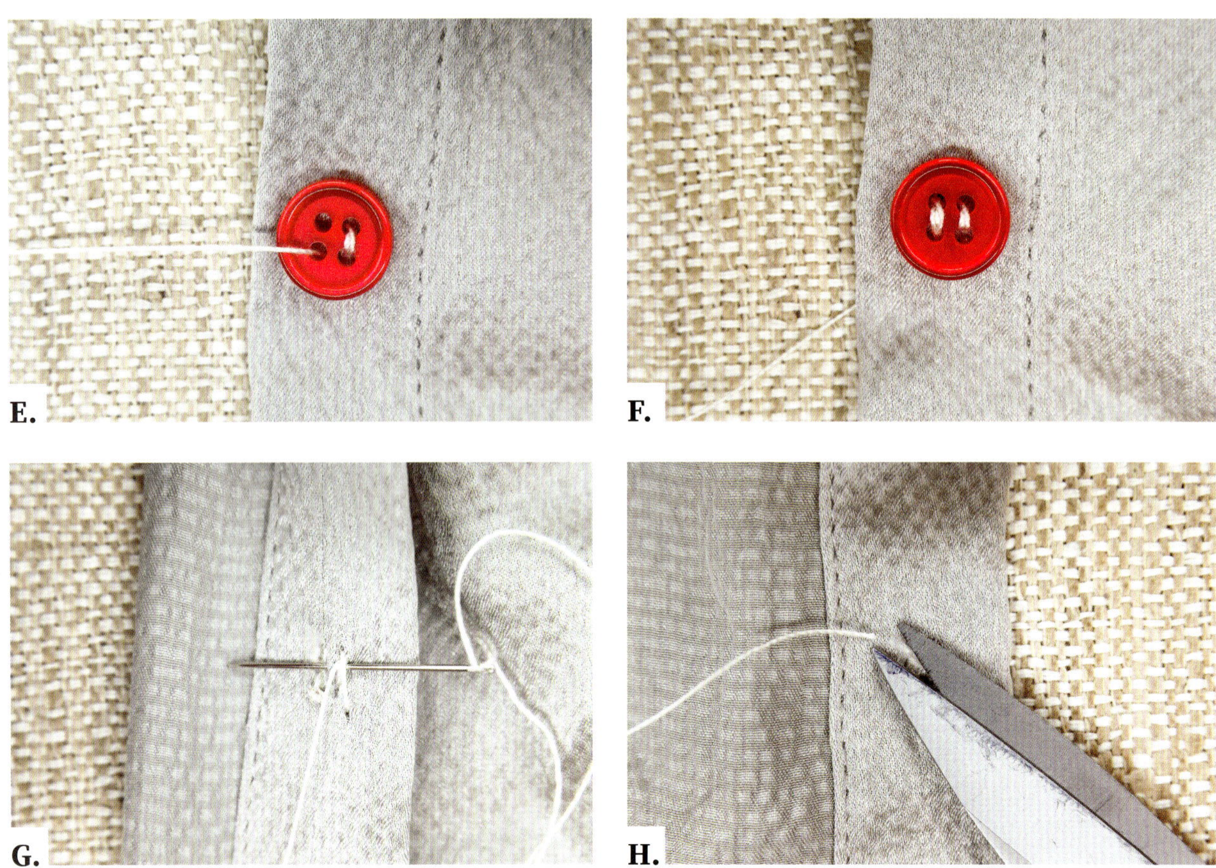

E.

F.

G.

H.

GIMME SOME SPACE

If the button is too snug to the surface of the fabric, it will not be able to pass through the buttonhole correctly and will come unbuttoned. This is especially true with thicker fabrics.

1. To fix this, place a second needle or a toothpick under the button while sewing to create space. *fig. A*
2. Once finished, remove the spacer and wrap the thread around the threads below the button several times and pull snug. *fig. B*
3. Insert the needle into the center of the wraps and out the back of the fabric. *fig. C*
4. Make a small tack stitch and knot the thread. Bury the thread tail in the fabric and trim off. *fig. D*

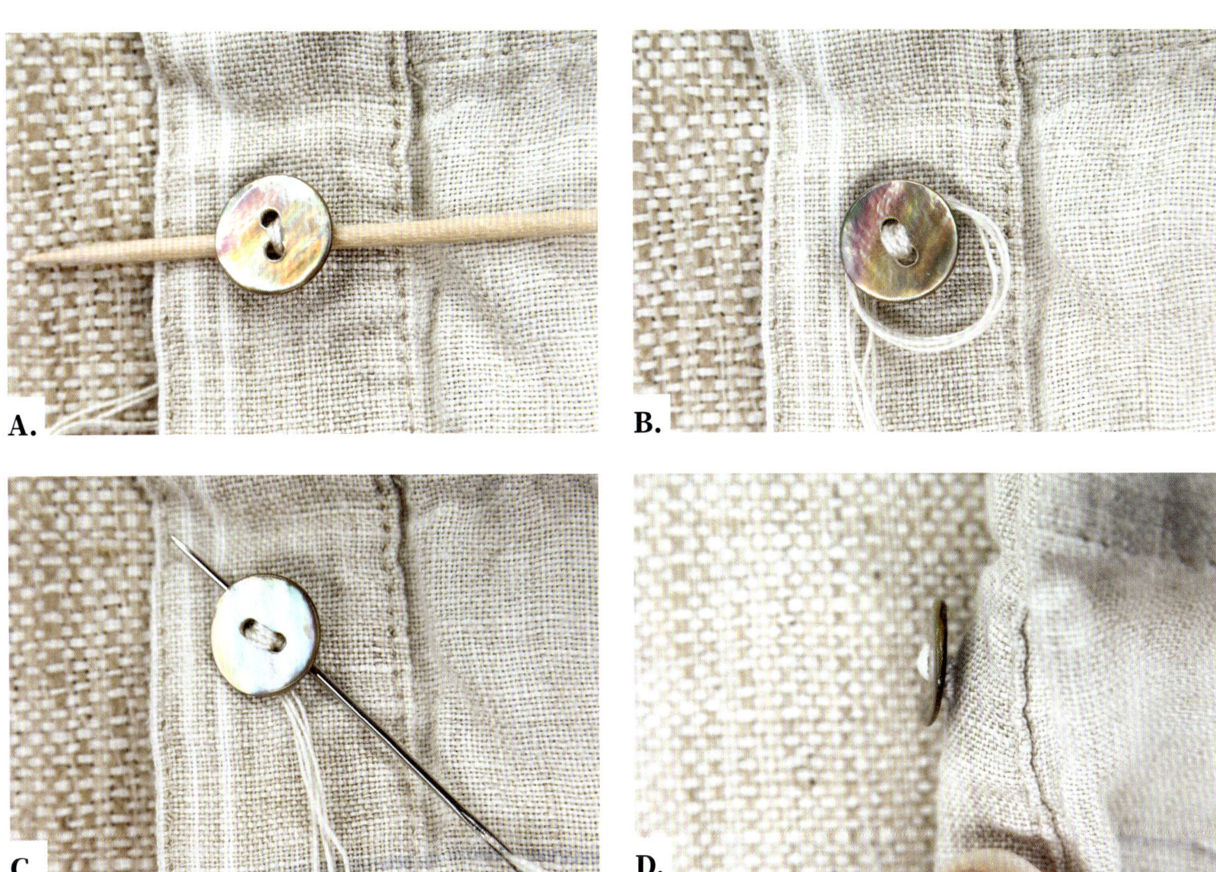

A. B. C. D.

Attach a Post Button

A post button does not lay flat to the fabric but, instead, has a raised back or post on it. The steps are basically the same as for a flat button with the stitches being made by passing the needle through the single hole of the post rather than multiple holes as for a flat button.

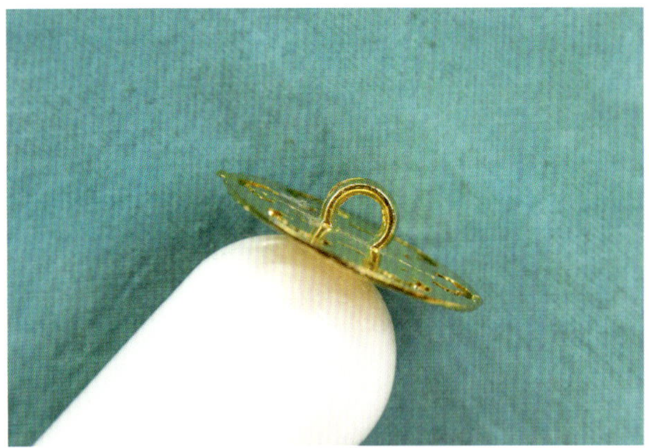

Snaps, Hook-and-Eye Closures, and Slider Clasps

Attaching snaps, hook-and-eye closures, and slider clasps is the same process as attaching flat buttons. Make sure the holes align with the previous placement and sew in place using a whipstitch (page 53).

In case of a lost snap or clasp, self-adhesive hook-and-loop dots are the quickest of quick fixes.

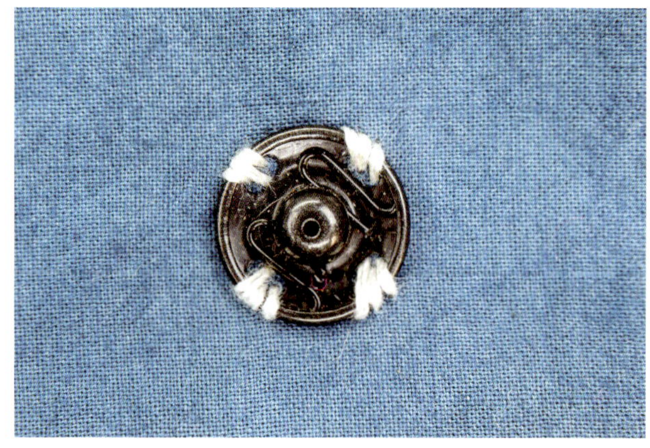

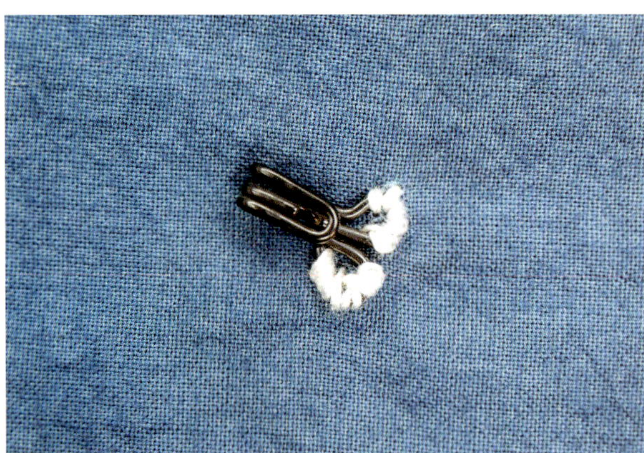

HEMMING

While there are any number of hemming stitches in the stitches section of this book, sometimes a popped hem needs a quick fix that can be dealt with later. Here are our favorite on-the-go options for a hem gone awry.

No-Sew Fixes

Steam-A-Seam (by The Warm Company) and other double-sided fusible webbing are great options if you have access to an iron. Apply to the inside of the hem and press with the iron to secure.

BONUS: Small pieces of fusible are good for applying to the back of a rip or tear to keep it from getting out of hand before a permanent mend can be made.

Temporary basting glue comes in small, portable packages that can fit into a purse or mending kit and will reattach a loose hem quickly. Simply wash out the glue when you are ready to permanently mend the hem.

Good old double-sided tape from the hardware store is a must for any mending kit and has saved us from flopping pant cuffs, trouser hems, and a skirt hem that met its match with a particularly vicious pair of leopard-print stiletto boots. Rip off a length and stick it between the separated layers, and you're back in business until a permanent mend can be made.

TIPS FOR SUCCESS

That We Couldn't Put Anywhere Else

These are our best tips and general notes that we wanted to include in this book but couldn't decide on the best place to put them. So, here they are in one tidy little spot. Enjoy!

STAB METHOD VS. SEWING METHOD (AND THE EXCEPTION TO THE RULE)

To stab or to sew? These are two terms applied to how stitches are made. And, as is most often the case, there is an exception to the rule.

The stab method of making stitches is for fabrics held taut in a hoop, thick fabric, or layered fabric. The needle is pushed into the fabric and drawn through before being inserted into the next point and pulled through again. This creates a stabbing motion.

The sewing method of making stitches is best for handheld fabrics or fabric that is more loosely held in the hoop. The more slack fabric allows the fabric to be lifted slightly enabling the needle to go into and out of the fabric in one movement.

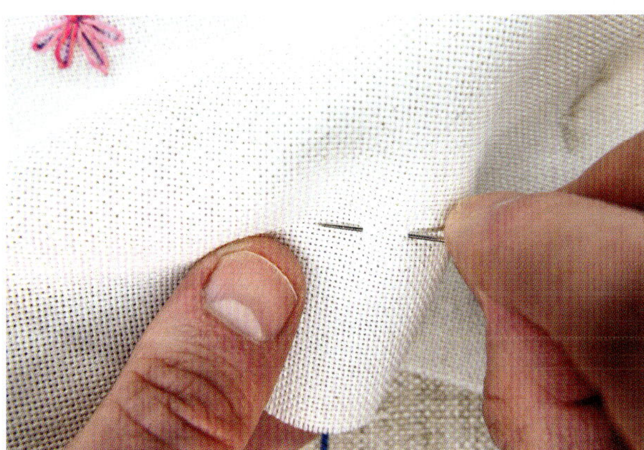

Often, the stab method is employed while learning the pattern of a stitch and then the sewing method is applied to all or part of the stitch where applicable, speeding up the process. A prime example of this is the feather stitch (page 66).

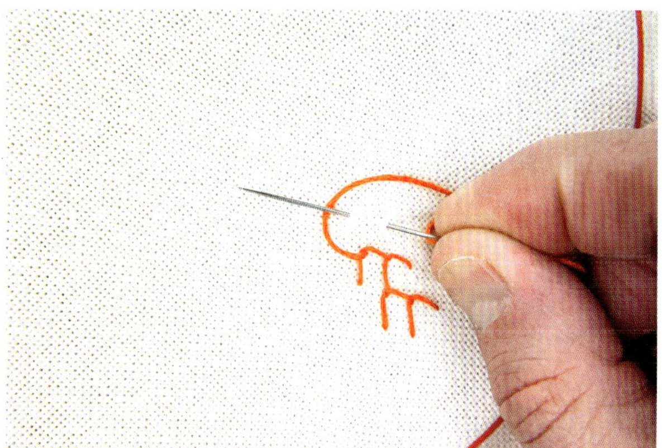

The exception to this stitching rule is the sashiko running stitch. Sashiko unshin is a motion of loading the fabric onto a needle and then pushing the needle through the fabric creating multiple stitches at a time (see Unshin: Handling the Needle, page 92). Once you learn this method for making running stitches, you won't want to go back to one stitch at a time.

MAKING A FORWARD STITCH VS. MAKING A BACKSTITCH

A forward stitch is advancing the needle from the starting point of stitching toward the ending point of the line of stitching.

A backstitch is moving the needle against the line of stitching toward the stitches previously made.

(DON'T) PUCKER UP!

Puckered fabric is the heartbreak of hand-stitchers and is caused by stitches that are tighter than the main fabric. Keep fabric and thread tension even (especially on backstitches and crossing stitches) by using a hoop to hold the fabric securely without stretching it. For hand-tensioned stitching, such as for sashiko and some knit mends, check the progress of the stitches often to ensure the stitches are laying evenly on the surface of the fabric.

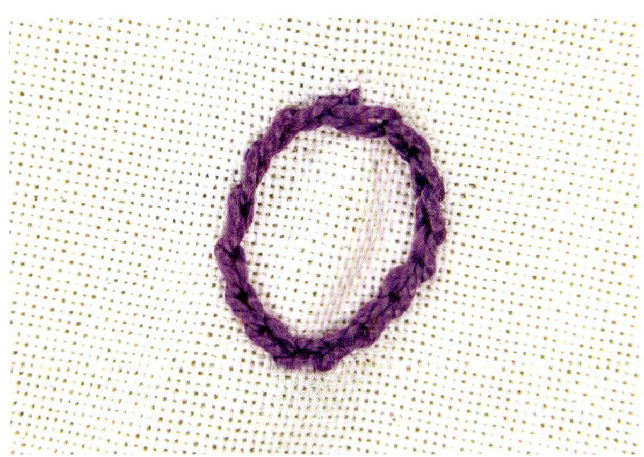

PRESSING VS. IRONING

Pressing means applying steady pressure directly downward with an iron or pressing tool.

Ironing means moving the iron around, such as for smoothing out large pieces of fabric or garments.

Pressing will set the thread on a seam, set the seam itself, or set the fabric squarely without moving the fabric around and stretching it out of shape. When pressing patches made from separate pieces, press squarely to avoid warped seams and joins.

YARN FOR MENDING

We like to keep a small variety pack of short lengths of yarn in our mending kit. This includes small hanks or balls of yarn from knitted and crocheted garments we have made, as well as a few spools of wool from Aurifil that fill in nicely for a variety of mends. And remember that weird little bundle of yarn that came with that sweater you bought? This is what it is for. Keep it and label it with the garment it came with. Bonus points: If the mend is needed on a gifted handmade item, see if the maker has any of that yarn left to create a mend. If you make a knit item, keep the extra yarn for future mends. Finally, remember that yarn is a great texture to add to your mends, so don't reserve it for just mending knit and crochet fabrics.

ABOUT THE AUTHORS

Shannon Roudhán and Jason Bowlsby are the dynamic DIY duo from Seattle, Washington. Their award-winning designs have been featured in and on the covers of domestic and international publications, and their craft, portrait, and fashion photography has appeared in books and magazines around the globe. Shannon & Jason have published fifteen books, including *Complete Crochet Course – the Ultimate Reference Guide, Designer Crochet, Boro & Sashiko: Harmonious Imperfection, Contemporary Kogin-zashi: Modern Sashiko Beyond Filling in the Gaps*, and *Scrappy Wonky Quilt Block Extravaganza,* which was released in June 2024.

The duo has been married for 31 years and have been teaching adults for 20+ years. They have a mastery of a variety of subjects, including boro and sashiko, crochet and knitting, sewing, quilting, photography, and embroidery. Their enthusiasm, quirky sense of humor, and relatable teaching style have made them sought after teachers in virtual, local, and national venues. Be sure to check out their selection of online classes on Craftsy, on Creative Spark, and through their own website, shannonandjason.com. The "edu-tainment" experience of a class with Shannon & Jason will leave you informed, empowered, and in stitches (see what we did there?).

Follow Shannon and Jason:
Online at shannonandjason.com
On Facebook, Instagram, and Pinterest at @embracethecreativechaos
On Patreon at @shannonandjason